'For I know the plans and *thoughts that I have for you,'* says the Lord, *'plans for peace* and *well-being and not for disaster to give you a future and a hope.'* – Jeremiah 29:11 (AMP)

So, go ahead. You already have My permission to win!

To:

_____

From:

_____

Date:

_____

PERMISSION TO Win

A DAUGHTER'S GUIDE TO WINNING FROM THE INSIDE OUT

THE WINNERS PRESS
WASHINGTON, DC

To the love, life, and legacy of my mother, First Lady Dorothy M. Hart. I love you. Thank you for your example of love, compassion, grace, and service. It's now my pleasure to share the gifts God has given me with women around the world.

To Beautiful Daughters everywhere.
You are brilliant beyond measure. May our coming together be a reminder that you have Permission To Win, you are never alone, and you have everything you need to play big, win even bigger, and create the legacy you desire. Now go get 'em!

ACKNOWLEDGMENTS

Kimberly D. recognizes and extends special appreciation to:

The Daughters of Legacy: Candice Camille, Veronica Wilson, Maria Stanfield, Tawanda Prince, Pamela Williams, Cassandra Dickerson, and Susan Kee. Thank you for trusting the God in me enough to come along and play. We didn't know it all, and it still remains to be seen what God has in store for us through our faith, unity, and commitment to serving others through our gifts. Continue to be the blessings that you are and to build those legacies that shall remain! *I love you!*

The Power Players, who took this opportunity to be the light and ran with it. You were chosen because of who you already are in the world. Don't lose sight of that, and never stop being the inspiration the next generation needs to see. *Much love to you all!*

William F. Hart, III, Bill Hart Photography (for PR and Photographer). Thank you for taking time to hear me out and for always exposing me to the best. You pulled me out of the bleachers and onto the field so I too could win. *Love you to Life, Big Brother!*

Jackie Hicks, CEO of Fond Memories Photography (for the Daughters of Legacy pictures). You heard, you saw, and you captured! Thank you so much for bringing your heart and gifts to this project. You and Letitia Thornhill, CEO of LetBeauty, LLC brought vision to life and escorted us to our next level. *Never the same!*

Dr. Reneé Starlynn Allen, The People's Emcee and Host of "The Renee Allen and Friends Show" on WLVS. Thank you for playing to win from the jump. You didn't hesitate to show up, lend a hand, extend your resources, and share anything else you thought I needed or should be aware of. You became my sister (our sister), and *we love you just because of who you are.*

BOOK CONTRIBUTORS

Register to receive your
FREE Downloadable
Permission To Win Workbook,
while available, at
PermissionToWinNow.com

CONTENTS

FOREWORD
By Nikki N. Klugh

Nikki Klugh Design Group, Inc., San Diego, CA
Full-Service Design
Everyday Luxurious Living Design Studio
Virtual Vision Sessions
Home Staging and Speaking

Just a few moments in one's lifetime can totally and unequivocally change a person's entire trajectory. I dare to say that a conversation I had with Kimberly D. Hart on March 21, 2014, was one of those moments for her.

Kimberly and I were casually talking during the VIP Mixer at the 2014 Get Radical Conference, when the conversation gradually became serious. I realized that God was setting us up. He allowed Kimberly to feel safe with me and open up about exactly what was holding her back from realizing her dreams. She began reciting a list of events that happened to her over the course of her life and how she felt as if the odds had been stacked against her.

God allowed me to be a willing vessel, although I had no advice to give, only questions to help her assess what it would take to move forward. At first, Kimberly had no answers, and then suddenly her hidden belief rose to the surface. Subconsciously, she no longer believed she had *permission to win.* The revelation not only exposed the deep, dark lies that had disheartened her and hindered her progress up to that point, but hearing it pierced her soul, opening up her eyes and lighting a fire under her that has since helped many women and young girls give themselves *permission to win!*

Ms. Hart is a *powerful* woman of God who was hiding her light under a bushel ... all because she had allowed a perception of a series of events to build a prison in which she chose to live. The enemy of our soul wanted to stifle her voice and thwart her calling. However, when God revealed the truth of her struggle and opened the doors to free her, she walked into a new reality, one that would usher in other daughters who are committed to emerge from the shadows of people, places, and things and step into the spotlight of their own divine destiny.

This book, *Permission To Win,* is the result of these powerful women coming together to help even more women and young girls walk in their God-given assignment. It shares stories from eight winning experts who, through the love and support of others and in the face of challenges, gave themselves *permission to win* and became the successful, powerful women they are today. Collectively, they identified other bright and intentionally successful women and girls to share tips and strategies they implemented for their own lives, who instead of being stuck in issues common to all of us, shifted gears and high-tailed it in the direction of their dreams and potential.

In the true spirit of service, Kimberly has provided for your easy access a glossary of key terms, a quick reference guide to help you get the inspiration you need for a particular topic or issue, opportunities to reflect and affirm your greatness, and information on how you can connect with the Daughters of Legacy and Queens to Bee Mentoring and Development Program for young ladies.

If you are that beautiful young girl, or even a woman (because there is a little girl in all of us who needs to be reminded every now and then she has *permission to win*) and you are ready to discover the winner inside you, position yourself to fulfill your dreams, make decisions that move you forward, press pass the obstacles and fears toward the promises of God for your life, and uncover the priceless treasures that surround you so you can play big and win from the inside out, then *Permission To Win* is the perfect place to begin. *Enjoy!*

SECTION ONE:

DEFINING MOMENTS WITH

THE DAUGHTERS
OF LEGACY

DON'T CALL IT
A COMEBACK!

By Kimberly D. Hart

"The Winning Strategist"
Speaker, Author, Motivator, Trainer
Master of Business Administration Degree

Founder and CEO, Kimberly D. Hart Consulting and Development Firm, The Daughters of Legacy, and Queens 2 Bee Mentoring and Development Program

Today, I know what it's like to be pressed on all sides, but not crushed; perplexed, but not in despair; persecuted, but not forsaken; struck down, but not destroyed. I thought I was setup to lose early in life, but, thank God, He had another plan. He allowed me to go through those difficult seasons to show me that no one dictates my ability to win but the one inside me. And, yes, it appeared that I was down and out for a really long time; however, now I realize I was just playing dead. Night and day, I gave in to the thoughts of others, and I let situations pollute my perception. However, I ignored statements such as: "You're a spoiled brat." "You're nothing but a show-off." "You think you can do whatever you want to do." "Here comes trouble." I allowed them to hover over me without addressing them. My aunt actually thought it was cute to buy me a t-shirt that commemorated this very thought. These statements and others took a toll on me simply because I didn't cast them down and deal with them as they occurred.

WAITING TO EXHALE

As a young girl from the Maryland suburbs, I was surrounded by a loving family, supportive neighbors (Hastings Drive/Seat Pleasant in the house), and a church home that gave me a place to discover my gifts and talents in a variety of ways. Back then, life was all about giving and being there for one another. I found so much pleasure in showing up for something greater than myself. It gave me value and a reason for being.

Being the daughter of a Bishop and First Lady allowed me to serve and explore different interests. I loved singing in the choir, ushering, planning events, assisting teachers, acting in plays, and working in the kitchen. I had to be the youngest person who knew how to skillfully batter chicken quarters, drop them in the deep fryer, take and fulfill orders from a hungry crowd after the morning's service. I even convinced my third-grade teacher, Mrs. Jones, to let me stay inside during recess to help her decorate the room, make copies, and prepare for the class to return.

I loved to serve, because it gave me a chance to operate in my gifts. It was like *breathing*. Not having this outlet will suffocate you, because your passions are energizing and must be used. In the process of living out loud, you'll discover the limitless possibilities that await you as you continue to breathe. Wow! That's living!

THE FIGHT IS FIXED: A PERFECT SACRIFICE

As time went on, I abruptly encountered events that shook this reality. Besides serving in the church choir, I participated in anything and everything I could, because so much life was in it and I was so creative. Soon, I would see the crowd growing cold and that the playing field wasn't as level as I once believed it to be. Around 10 years old, I entered the church's King and Queen Contest. My brother and I both ran for the royal court. When we took on a project, our mother was relentless in making sure we did our best. Well, the time finally came when a new King and Queen would reign. The king was announced, and my brother took the throne. The same was announced for the Queen, but I was the Runner-Up. I can't tell you how disappointed I was, not only because I wasn't queen, but also because I knew how much my brother would taunt me with the new TV he won. You see, he was the type who would take the TV into the bathroom to make sure I didn't watch it. Not much has changed, but the contest itself was definitely an eye opener. I soon learned that my brother and I both raised the most money. Then how on earth did he become King and I become runner-up? My mother finally told me "they" decided to let someone else win, because we were both in the same household. How would it have looked if the two children of the pastor won the contest and took home the two TVs? If you had asked me, it would have looked like they did the most work to earn the prizes. I couldn't believe it, and for some strange reason they expected me to understand. They obviously thought I should be ok with second place, but I was more concerned about how they made the decision as to who would be the winner and who would be the sacrifice. That night I realized I didn't have *permission to win* the crown, and it haunted me for years to come.

NOT THE RIGHT TYPE!

A few years later, I was recommended to audition for a new tour production of the stage play "Annie." I decided to go for it, because I was no stranger to acting, singing, and dancing. I practiced long and hard into the wee hours of the nights leading up to the audition. I was ready! When the time came, I took center stage, faced the panel of experts, told them I was auditioning for the role of Annie, and sung the movie's classic, "Tomorrow." By the time I was finished, the panel gave me a standing ovation. I addressed their questions and left only to be met by a reporter and TV crew who wanted to interview me for the nightly news. He asked me where I got that big powerful voice for such a little lady. I told him that I studied hard and came to give it all I had. He congratulated me, and I went off to wait for the call. Several days later, we got the call. The woman said they were highly impressed with my performance, *but* I didn't have the right "look" for the character of Annie. She continued to congratulate me and my mother, and talked about other roles for which I should consider auditioning.

Of course, they were looking for a little Caucasian girl. As silly as it may sound, I never thought about that. I knew I was a young Black girl with curly hair, but it never crossed my mind that I wouldn't have a fair shot at the role. If I had thought about it, I probably would have never tried out for the part. It was at that moment that I realized I didn't have *permission to win* the role.

POSITION FILLED

By the time I was a teenager, I was even more confident in my gifts, talents, and abilities. The Miss Achievement Pageant was coming up, and I wanted to compete. Needless to say, I practiced day and night for months, because I enjoyed the arts. Finally, I was involved with something that would be based solely on my skills. It was simply up to me to "bring it," and I liked knowing that the position was fair game. I was never afraid of losing as long as I had a fair shot at winning. This was my Miss America Pageant and a stepping stone to greater opportunities.

The time for the main event arrived, and I was ready for sound check. My mother chose a classic song by Mahalia Jackson, "Somebody Bigger Than You," and my brother Billy played the piano for me. As I bellowed the finale, the crowd rose to their feet. I looked into the cheering crowd, took another bow, and exited stage right with total confidence that I had nailed it. All my hard work finally paid off, and I felt right at home.

The night was coming to a close, and the third-place winner was announced. The remaining contestants clutched hands across the stage, for it was time for the runner-up. "Drumroll, please." Suddenly, the crowd gasped for air. "Kimberly Hart, come on down." I was so excited to place in what was the toughest competition of my life. I gave the classic princess wave and went stage left to receive my flowers and trophy. The applause continued, but now it was time to find out who would be the lucky girl taking home the crown. The name was called, and for some reason I was a little shocked. The judges chose the director's daughter over all the other amazing contestants who really rocked the stage that night. Wow! I felt some kind of way, but the whole experience was incredible for me; besides, I was the "Runner-Up."

I was worn out but ready to go celebrate with those who came to support me. The dressing room was packed with contestants, family members, and guests rushing in to congratulate us all. As I grabbed my things, I overheard my mother say, "Ah, that's ok—she's fine." I didn't know what she was talking about, so I focused on getting the rest of my things. As we started to walk out, I overheard other parents telling my mother that they robbed me. They huddled around her trying to motivate her to stand up for me. In true Dorothy Hart fashion, she was not going to make a big deal out of it there.

The next day, I overheard my mother talking about the competition to someone. They mentioned the relation-ship the director had with the so-called judges and how everyone felt the competition had been rigged so that her daughter was featured in the newspaper and magazine articles—not to mention her name was already on the trophy. Duh! I sat there in the basement holding my second-place trophy thinking, "Wow. They already knew who the winner would be." I never really could have won the competition. For the first time in all those months leading up to the event, I felt that it was all a fake. All my hard work was for nothing. I finally asked my mother if what they said was true, and she said, yes, but she was so proud of me. I had showed up and had given 1,000 percent—that was enough. What she didn't know is that I was sick and tired of hearing that. All through my life, I was realizing that working hard and giving my all was truly not enough.

STOLEN IDENTITY

Leaving entertainment behind, I drew close to my first love—ministry, which was not just a place I went to only on Sunday mornings and Tuesday nights. Ministry was a way of life; therefore, it became who I was and who I am. I grew up serving wherever I was needed in the church, which gave me opportunities to nurture my gifts and talents. As long as I was serving others, everything was fine. The challenges came when I wanted to be, do, and give more—then the daggers came flying from people who I thought had my back. If nothing else, I thought these people wanted me to be my best. However, singing in the choir was fine, as long as I didn't run for choir president or step out front to lead a song. Helping the ministries have successful events was great until I started writing my own plays and producing events. As long as I played small and served as the *runner-up*, I was welcomed. The moment I allowed what was in me to come forth, the deal was off. I was hurt and confused. The people I had known for years were suddenly asking me, "Who do you think you are?" In other words, "What makes you think you have *permission to win?*" Sadly to say, by now I couldn't answer them.

A PLACE TO CALL MY OWN

I retreated to a place that gave me the peace I was looking for, where there were no expectations outside of those I placed on myself, and where I could soar to heights that were comfortable for me. I was finally in control of winning from where I was, and no one could stop me. This place was where I spent time with the only person I could depend on, and it was refreshing. I could be real with myself. I could admit that I didn't have *permission to win,* and no one was there trying to convince me otherwise. No more lies or false hopes surrounded me there. For the first time, I was in control of my mental and spiritual well-being. Most importantly, I was sick and tired of being hurt. I was bruised from the constant battles, and I didn't feel like making excuses. In this place, I didn't have to fight, show up, pretend that I cared, or meet anyone's expectations. I was safe, out of the spotlight, and selective in what I allowed myself to be involved with, making sure whatever I chose, I was able to win in my own little way. I was finally at peace as the *runner-up.* What I didn't realize for years to come is that this safe, cozy, intimate, secluded place was actually a grave.

KIMBERLY, COME FORTH!

I was slowly dying year after year, growing weaker in confidence, and losing my voice and connection to the world around me. Although I was at peace as it related to the world, my frustration with myself grew more and more. I wasn't fulfilling my purpose for being here. To be truthful, I wasn't doing much of anything. I stayed under the radar to keep from rocking any boats. I accomplished some personal goals, such as getting my MBA and purchasing an apartment building, but I was still unfulfilled and slowly dying. I grew cynical about those who were showing up big in their life, not just anyone doing big things, but those who authentically were living from the inside out. I knew that feeling—I could smell it and spot it a mile away. I could see it in their eyes as they came across my path or appeared across the screen. There's something uniquely amazing and breathtaking about someone who is powerfully living from the inside out, and it was calling my name.

In 2014, I felt a shift happening in me. By now, I knew that I was being called out of hiding and commanded to go forward. I had to learn to trust God and not man. He challenged me by saying, "You do have *permission to win!*" He assured me that He was going to walk with me through the shadows of death where I had accepted the lies as my truth and where I started living based on my feelings (which was a huge mistake and one that I'm learning to overcome even now). Trusting His love for me was the first order of business. Believing what He said to me and about me was the start of a deeper relationship with Him. The Light of Truth was breaking forth to resuscitate my dead, stinking thinking, and I knew that this was the only way I would ever *breathe* again.

I CHOOSE TO WIN

Looking back over my life, I can see how strategically important those challenges were to my destiny. I learned winning comes from within, and it doesn't require anyone's permission. If God put greatness inside me, then greatness is who I am and I had no right to play dead. Even when people don't "get you," keep pushing and looking for more opportunities to be your best. As you can see, that may take some time, but never give up on yourself. That's where the frustration comes from. Passion, gifts, and talents are energy, they are alive, and they will not stop calling you until you answer them. I thought I could settle into a place called mediocrity to keep the peace, but even there, the winner inside, who refused to play dead with me, tormented me. So, you see, it's not a comeback, because greatness never goes away.

It's time for you step up to the plate of your life. Playing small for whatever reason is not acceptable, especially if it's to appease the insecurities of others. God has given you a purpose and a dream that He expects you to fulfill. This includes overcoming the challenges of your past, your present, and your future. They are there to prove to you and the world who you are. Don't shrink back, play dead, settle for less, or lie to yourself. Instead, let your opinion of you outweigh the opinions of others. Pay attention to the stories you are telling yourself. Trust that you already have the answers to your questions. Be comfortable in knowing that not everyone can "take" you. Believe in your dreams, and always be willing to play and win big from the inside out!

The next time someone asks you, "Who in the world do you think you are?" … tell them!

DESTINED TO BE
QUEEN

By Tawanda Prince

"The Good Life Coach and Author"
Daughters of Legacy, Winning in Vision
Master of Arts, Teaching
Former Host/Executive Producer of Faith Café Radio

Founder, Sisters in the Faith and The Rising Stars Girls'
Mentoring Program
thegoodlifecoach.net

The day had finally arrived, and what a special day it was—the NAACP Cotillion of our local chapter. Lots of preparation had been made, and anticipation was high. Yes, the day had finally come, and I was so excited about it. This was my time to shine, and I was looking forward to it.

Wow! The time had gone by so quickly. It seemed like just yesterday that we had the first interest meeting, and now it was show time. Being a debutante was not all glitz and glamour; a lot of hard work went into it. First, I had to choose a Lady-in-Waiting who would be my support person. Then, of course, I had to find an escort, a favorite boy who would help present me to society as a debutante. Of course, there was also the dress. Oh, yes, the dress was of major importance. Then, many weeks of practice, practice, practice were in order. We had to learn the proper way to walk, sit, stand, and curtsy. Also, we had to master several formations, dances, and routines. We were all in competition to be crowned the Queen.

CALLING ALL QUEENS

Being the Queen was the ultimate goal of each girl in the cotillion. The Queen would receive flowers, scholarship money, a trophy, a beautiful crown, and the honor of representing the organization at community events and presiding over the cotillion the following year to crown the next Queen. Certainly, it was every participant's dream to be the Queen. I, too, set my sights on winning. The Queen position was based on which girl sold the most tickets to the ball. I gave myself *permission to win* by taking on this mission full-swing. My parents and I worked extremely hard to sell those tickets as well as sell advertisements for the cotillion booklet. My mother was a member of the local chapter, and she worked closely with the members on several projects and events. We asked everyone we knew to support my mission to be the Queen in one way or another. I worked hard and tracked my progress weekly. There were 20 to 25 debutantes, and the competition was tight.

PREPARED FOR THE THRONE

At age 14, I did not quite understand the full value of the work of the organization, but my parents were raising me to offer service to my community and society at large. Lots of good work was being done, and I was part of that movement in the 1970s. This cotillion was to be the highlight of our participation in the organization. So, as we made the final preparations for the ball, the excitement mounted. My Aunt was my Lady-in-Waiting, and a family friend's son was my handsome escort. My aunt who designed and made my mother's wedding gown designed and made my beautiful white gown. My dad was in place to present me to my escort. I had my first manicure, my hair was done beautifully, and I was ready to be the Queen.

According to the latest ticket sales tally, I led the pack. The ball finally arrived, and I was on my way. Not only was I being presented to society as a debutante, but I was also making a statement to family and friends that I was a young lady moving up to the next level in my life. I was showing everyone that I had set goals and worked hard to achieve them. I was going to show the world who I was.

AND THE WINNER IS ...

The night was magical indeed. All of our practice paid off, and it was a beautiful cotillion. The debutantes were fabulous, the routines were flawless, and the Queen was ready to be crowned. The winning court was finally announced, and I was declared...the First Runner-Up. *What? First Runner-Up? How could that be? I had worked so hard.*

The final count showed that I was the winner, so what happened? It turns out that the young lady who was crowned Queen sold one more ticket than I did; her mother *also* happened to be on the cotillion committee. So, I was crowned First Runner-Up and, of course, was told that if the Queen should somehow not be able to fulfill her duties, I would step into that spot. I was disappointed, but I knew that I had done my best. I learned that sometimes life can be unfair, but I must still always give it my best shot. Tears flowed, I accepted my position.

THE SECOND TIME AROUND

Let's fast-forward to the next year's cotillion. I put all of the previous year's drama behind me and moved on to whatever else life held for me. Surprisingly, we were notified that the young lady who was crowned Queen was unable to attend the cotillion and that I would be the one to crown the new Queen. So, there it was. I was declared the Queen. I was going to get my chance to shine after all.

I was destined to be Queen! Delay is not denial. Although I was not initially crowned as the Queen, I was ultimately given the opportunity to reign. It was another glorious cotillion. The next group of debutantes was spectacular, and I had the esteemed honor of crowning the new Queen. My picture was also in the newspaper representing me as the Queen of the court from the previous year.

WELCOME TO THE GOOD LIFE

Wow! What a comeback! I gave myself *permission to win* by operating in integrity and honesty, and working hard toward my goal. What truly made me the Queen was that I maintained grace and a winning spirit and attitude, even when I had been treated unfairly.

That same winning spirit that has permitted me to experience success as an author, speaker, teacher, and life coach. I have applied this and other life lessons in order to accomplish my goals of writing and publishing several books, writing and producing plays, and, most importantly, teaching and coaching others to live their lives to the fullest, as The Good Life Coach.

As you journey through life, you will encounter situations in which you are treated unfairly or you are cheated out of something that is rightfully yours. You will also encounter people who challenge you and try to use their influence to affect your outcomes negatively. You must remember that your character will always speak for itself; it will either speak well of you or badly of you. Give yourself *permission to win* by doing the right thing regardless of what others are doing. I believe you can never go wrong when you do the right thing. You will always wear a crown of glory when you keep a winning attitude, no matter what the scoreboard says.

Winning starts with a winning spirit, and if you have a winning spirit, you are destined to be Queen in everything that you do.

PERMISSION TO WIN

VALUES
TO LIVE BY

By Veronica T. Wilson

Daughters of Legacy, Winning in Purpose
Senior Managing Consultant at IBM Global Services
Owner and Coach, Crimson Heat All Stars
CEO, GoBeyond Coaching and Mentoring
www.crimsonheat.com

Born in Demopolis, Alabama, located just a few miles west of historic Selma, I grew up in a small three-bedroom flat with my grandmother, my grandfather, my teenage mother, an uncle, and a host of cousins. My grandmother, the late Mattie Lee Wilson, was a cook at the local diner, and my grandfather was a truck driver. Faith, family, and service to others were the cornerstones of our household. My grandmother instilled these core values in us when we were very young, and she demonstrated them daily.

I still remember sleeping on rollaway beds in the living room with four other cousins—three at the head of the bed and two at the foot. All of the bedrooms were filled with other family members. I remember dinner time when my grandmother would fry up a whole chicken, and each of us would lay claim to a specific part of the chicken. I also remember my grandmother's homemade jams, jellies, and sweet potato pies, which she shared with those who stopped by the house. We learned early how to share, sacrifice, and be of service to others.

Much of my childhood was spent inside the church; we spent as much time there as we did at home. Sundays were literally like full days of work! We attended Sunday School, Baptist Training Union, morning service, afternoon service, and then evening service on most Sundays. My grandmother was very active in the church, serving in many of the ministries over the years before eventually becoming the Mother of the Church. She was truly a hard worker and was dedicated to serving others. She used to say, "I may be old, but I am not dead. I can still contribute." She made sure we were active in the church, too. I served on the Youth Choir, the Junior Usher Board, the Mass Choir, and the Junior Quartet. I still feel a little tickle in my throat every time I go into the church, as I think about those soft peppermints my grandmother used to give us when we were young to keep us quiet and the "boomerang eye" she threw at us if we were misbehaving. She didn't have to say a word—she gave us that look, and instantly we knew to stop what we were doing and fix it immediately.

I share all of this about my past so you can understand how all of these experiences contributed to the woman that I am today. I stand on a *faith* foundation that those long hours spent in church during my childhood fortified. Like my grandmother, I work hard and sacrifice much to leave a legacy for my nieces and nephews. I understand and embrace the connection between service and success, because I am the product of it.

Through my meager beginnings, I was tooled with a suite of values that have proven invaluable in my life and on my career journey. I, too, am a believer that it doesn't matter how you start; it only matters how you finish! Regardless of the obstacles life has thrown at me, and I have had more than a few (I'll tell you more in my next book), I have always had faith to stand on, family to retreat to, and the seeds of service to fall back upon. As young ladies who have the whole world in front of you, I believe it's important for you to *Ground* yourselves, *Surround* yourselves, and *Profound* yourselves.

GROUND YOURSELF

Life gets tough sometimes, and we all need a place where we can go to feel safe, to regroup, and to be renewed. I am talking about that place where you can go when the chips are down and your back is against the wall; that place where you can be frail and imperfect. For me, that place is my *Faith*. The lyrics to one of my favorite gospel hymns, "My Hope is Built" really capture my grounding best:

> *My hope is built on nothing less than Jesus' blood and righteousness;*
> *I dare not trust the sweetest frame, but wholly lean on Jesus' name.*
> *On Christ, the solid rock, I stand; all other ground is sinking sand. All other ground is sinking sand.*

I remember being frustrated with the long hours spent in the car driving from church to church; with the *long* sermons that always ended with people crying; and those awful chicken dinners every church served at the end of service. While I was frustrated (as a child and an infant in *Faith*), I am now grounded by the very words those songs and sermons put inside of me. I learned to turn to a Source called Jesus, a tool called the Bible, and a weapon called prayer to get me through difficult times.

I can say that the year 2000 was one of the most difficult years of my life. I was in the middle of getting divorced from my husband of seven years. I was in the middle of a complete career change and in the process of starting my business, Crimson Heat All Stars, Inc. It was a very stressful, confusing, and important season of change, though I didn't recognize it as such at the time. I was emotionally vulnerable. So, naturally when my estranged father called to tell me he wanted to meet me, I was elated! I was so excited to hear his voice on the phone: "Baby Girl, your daddy is in town, and I really want to see you." Wow! After 28 years, I finally get to meet and spend time with my father. This was a positive turn, the light I needed during a very dark time … or so I thought.

As I've shared, I was in the middle of a divorce and in the process of moving out of "his" house. I had taken every material thing "I" owned and stuffed them inside my car, a car which I had only had for about 30 days (it still had paper tags). My father asked to use my car to drive to his friend's house, because he was having car trouble. Never did I imagine that the same day my father came back into my life, he would walk back out of my life, with my car and everything that I owned. There I stood, alone, 1,100 miles away from my family. I had *nothing!* I lost everything in that single decision. I was *devastated!* In that moment, all I could do was stay grounded in my *Faith!* My prayers comforted me, and my Faith gave me hope—it sustained me, it guided me, and it protected me.

I know it was God Who brought me out of 2000 and has kept me during my IBM-career and with my business for the last 16 years! It was also that same Faith in God that helped me to forgive my father. I do not live with anger or malice in my heart. Through that experience, I learned how to trust God in a whole new way. I also learned a lot about myself—Veronica. I learned about my own inner strength and resolve, and how to push through whatever life throws my way.

For me, it's my Faith in God that's my grounding. For you, it could be family or friends, fitness, or your own inner strength. Whatever your source is, you have to ground yourself with it. By grounding yourself, you will have a place on which to land and to stand when life knocks you down. *Ground yourself!*

SURROUND YOURSELF

Anyone who has ever attended a Crimson Heat competition has witnessed the massive crowd of people dressed in their red shirts, has heard the thunder of the drums beating, and has listened to the people chanting *Heat! Clap, Clap, Heat!* These are the people who surround our children in the competition and cover them. They cultivate a climate for our children in which to flourish in the competition arena. They set the atmosphere and calm the children's spirits. The children are reminded that they have a family of supporters out there waiting to see their performance. Essentially, they are the *"cheerleaders"* for the cheerleaders.

You need to surround yourself with your own cheerleaders, those who will believe in you and support you through the highs and the lows. Every one of us needs people around us who will tap us on the shoulder and tell us when we are right and when we are wrong. I'm talking about those who will help you when you steer off course. Find the ones who will walk with you blindly and trust you wholeheartedly—your ride-or-die chicks!

Thinking about it reminded me of the year 2007 when I lost the woman who taught me everything about Faith, Family, Service, and Life. Everything I know about being a good human being, I learned from my grandmother, Mattie Lee Wilson, God rest her soul. She was so proud of me for creating a gym and for working with children and dedicating my life to serving others. I made many promises to her that she would one day get to see my teams perform. Tired of promising, I finally committed and scheduled my teams to perform in Birmingham, Alabama, in the Crimson Classic. I loaded three buses with people, and we traveled from Washington, DC, to Birmingham. I was so excited! Finally, my grandmother could see what I had accomplished. She could finally see the thing that kept me from so many holidays and family events. I was so excited about this moment, and all I wanted was for her to be proud of me as she watched the children perform.

Unfortunately, on the very day we arrived, she passed away. She was not able to see the teams perform in Birmingham; instead she watched the performances from Heaven. The thing that stood out most for me was the circle that the children, coaches, and parents formed around me that day as they said a prayer asking God to comfort and cover me. It was in that moment that I knew my Grandmother's transition happened in divine order. I was surrounded by people who loved me and who she knew would take care of me. I was in good hands, so now she could let go.

It is important that you always surround yourself with folks who will be there, no matter what; folks who will stand with you, pray for you, lift you when you fall down, and correct you when you steer off course. *Surround yourself with them!*

PROFOUND YOURSELF

How many of you have heard something so powerful and compelling that it made you move? It made you think about things in a new way, or it made you act differently, or shift and move in a new direction. It was profound, in the traditional sense of the word. I'm going to violate grammar and use the word "profound" in a way that is not traditional—as a verb—so bear with me on this.

We each have a voice that exists deep inside us. We are born with it. Some call it intuition, internal instincts, gut feelings, or a moral compass. Regardless of what you choose to call it, the reality is, if we really got in touch with that voice, listened to it, and acted upon it, our lives would be fundamentally different. I believe that quiet, soft voice that lives inside each of us is God's gift to help us navigate through life. It was given to us to lead us and guide us in the right direction. Whenever I find myself in doubt or worry, or simply at a decision point, I have learned to go to a quiet place and be still so I can hear that inner voice speak so clearly and sweetly to me. I have learned over time that the voice is the most profound sound that I could ever hear. It tells me when I am right and when I am wrong; when I need to move and when I need to be still. Now, don't get me wrong. At times I listen, and at times I don't, but I have found that every time I did not listen to that voice, things did not go as I thought they would.

When I was toiling over the decision to leave Fairfax County Government to join IBM, I found myself up at night, unsure of what to do. Over and over, night after night, I wrestled with the decision. "It's 100 percent travel. How will I be able to run my business and be on the road all of the time?" All of these questions danced in my mind. Finally, I was driving from work one day, heading to Greenbelt, Maryland, from Fairfax, Virginia. That was a long drive, to say the very least. I decided to turn off the radio and just focus intently on what my inner voice was saying about this decision. I was about eight miles into my Route 66 East journey when, clear as day, I heard the most profound words spoken to me: *"Opportunity only knocks once; when it knocks on the door, you better walk in."*

Startled by the clarity and strength of the voice, I pulled over on the side of the road. I was shaken up a bit. The voice was louder, clearer, and sterner than it had ever been before. It was obvious to me that this was the answer for which I had been searching. When I finally got home, I immediately logged on to the IBM website to submit my paperwork. On the main screen of the Human Resources page was a large door on which these words were inscribed: "Your Opportunity Awaits." Underneath the door was the question: "Will you walk in?"

I almost fainted! Literally, it took my breath away. Here was the opportunity that voice had spoken of, and in that moment, all the doubt, worry, and uncertainty instantly faded. I would have never been able to experience such an epiphany had I not become one with my inner voice. You have to allow the voice that lives inside you to become the most *Profound* thing that you hear and to which you respond. Get in touch and in tune with it. Listen intently to it, and trust it to guide your path! Yes, *Profound yourself.*

It is now your charge to *Ground* yourself, *Surround* yourself, and *Profound* yourself. *Ground* yourself in something on which you can stand when life knocks you down. *Surround* yourself with people who will pour into you, who will support you, and who will be there for you when times are hard. *Profound* yourself—make your inner voice the most profound thing you hear! Tap into it, trust it, and act on it. When in doubt, don't move! Be still, get quiet, and wait for your inner voice to speak. It will assure you that you have *permission to win.*

I can assure you, based upon my own life, that if you do those three things, you can survive anything life throws at you, because you are *strong and powerful.* Walk and Soar!

God, bless you all, my Beautiful, Powerful, and Gifted Daughters.

SUCCESS:
THE BEST REVENGE

By Candice Camille

"The Wellologist"
Daughters of Legacy, Winning in Health & Wellness
CEO, Candice Camille Enterprises
Pure Nuphoria Wellness Space
Think Well, Be Well Now
www.candicecamille.com

Winning and succeeding in the face of adversity are things you have to want, feel, and fight like hell for. It's a mind thing, and you get to decide if this defines you, destroys you, or makes you stronger. Often, we are tested, not to show our weaknesses, but to discover what we are made of and how strong and powerful we really are. I had to fight my way through some remarkable battles in life. Malcolm X said it best: *"There is nothing better than adversity. Every defeat, every heartbreak, every loss, contains its own seed, its own lesson on how to improve your performance next time."*

Looking back, I realize that life is 10 percent chance and 90 percent attitude. That means 10 percent of life is what happens to you, while the other 90 percent is about how you respond to it. Giving yourself *permission to win* is all about how you respond.

STARS IN MY EYES

Growing up, I was a young upwardly bound student in the gifted and talented program in the Newark, New Jersey, Public School System. I was headed toward a career in aerodynamics. Back then, studying math and science was my thing. I wanted to be an Astronaut. I could see myself blasting off into space, bursting through the stars, while watching the Earth's surface diminish with each new altitude. All I can say about that is God has a sense of humor, because *things didn't turn out quite the way I planned.*

Like with most of us, life takes some unexpected twists and turns. I endured child abuse and molestation, single parenthood, homelessness, obesity, and domestic violence. Instead of flying high above the clouds, I bobbed and weaved real-life blows in the streets. I'm glad to say I survived those struggles and thankfully landed firmly on my feet. More importantly, I can see how many of my setbacks were simply setting me up to be stronger, enabling me to position myself to overcome some of the biggest challenges I would face in my life.

SUDDEN SETBACKS

One of the meanest monsters I have ever had to face was tracheal (throat) cancer—yes, the "C" word. During this challenging time in my life, I took heed to what my doctor advised me to do; however, I also studied a holistic and natural approach to healing my body. I discovered the only way to make my body strong and whole was through good nutrition and movement. Physical movement has become a source of extreme power for me. Having the ability to think and be well isn't something you inherit or something that is given to you. It is a conscious choice or decision that you make for the rest of your life. Wellness became my state of mind, and it wasn't something I just did every now and then. It was who I became, hence "The Wellologist."

Life was good; being healthy and teaching it to others became my purpose, and I was fueled with so much passion around it that I fired my boss and found a business partner with which to go at it full steam ahead. We had similar dreams about growing the business, so I took everything I had financially, physically, mentally, and emotionally and threw it into building this dream business. I had thought my biggest comeback was kicking cancer's behind, and then Murphy's Law went into effect. Whatever could go wrong, did! *Things didn't turn out quite the way I planned.*

TOSSED TO AND FRO

The business was up and running, and things were going really well, or so I thought. Something just wasn't clicking between my business partner and me. We had the same vision ... didn't we? We both wanted this to work and to be profitable ... didn't we? Our personalities were so different, but we could complement each other ... couldn't we?

Question after question came to my mind, and truthfully, I didn't have the heart to hear the truth. One of us was looking at the business as a viable part of life, while the other was looking at it as a hobby. We soon realized that we were not a good fit at all, because we fought constantly!

Often, you are so focused on the dream and you want it to succeed so badly that you start ignoring the warning signs and your gut feelings that are telling you it's not working. When your intuition begins to nudge you, please pay attention. Give it room to speak to you, and listen up. I was so hard-headed that I kept going when it was screaming for me to let go.

It all finally came to a head in an explosive way. Right when I thought I had ended all the horrific events in my life, here I was being caught right back in the vortex of another storm. If I had to describe it, I would call it a tsunami. I was literally being pushed and pulled to and fro from the depths of my soul. My dreams, for which I worked so hard, were vastly becoming a nightmare. I truthfully had an incredible vision for the business, *but things didn't turn out quite the way I planned.*

A VIEW FROM THE PIT

At that moment, my life came to a screeching halt. I found myself in the midst of a business divorce. I got really angry, and just like any other divorce, it got really ugly! I thought I was fighting for my life, but in the end, it turned out to be just "stuff."

I had exhausted all of my money to the point where I couldn't fulfill my basic needs. I had nothing to eat, but a few slices of molded bread and some jelly. I had to ask myself if I could actually eat that molded bread, and if so, would it kill me. I was too hungry not to eat it and found out that it didn't kill me. I took that route because of my ego, having too much pride to call anyone for help. I wouldn't dare tell them of my destitute situation. My whole life was being snatched away from me, and it took me back to that place of homelessness where I fought for my life. In this place, I wasn't thinking of just reacting; I was in survival mode.

I had to make a decision, and my response had to count. My mind during the day told me to fight for the dream, while at night my reality was the source of all my pain. I felt like the people in my life had turned against me—my family, my friends, my business associates, and partners. I felt no one really cared if I lived or died. I was operating business as usual in the day, becoming very good at masking my pain, if I do say so myself (in my Jay Z voice). Oh, but when I was alone, the weight of the world pinned me down for the count, because I was too embarrassed and too afraid of being judged, which only prolonged my devastation. Although, I put on a front during the daytime hours, I knew that it would eventually come to a head, because *things didn't turn out quite the way I planned.*

A DESPERATE SURRENDER

Slowly, but surely, I lost my will to fight. During the night, I heard voices in my mind telling me to hurt myself. They said, "Enough is enough already. How much more of this can you take?" However, no matter what the voices said to me, I held on to what I knew about God and to the few Bible Scriptures I knew. They gave me strength to operate during the day, but of course it was back to the battlefield of the mind at night.

One long and deeply lonely night, the walls seemed to be closing in on me. The room got smaller and smaller and darker and darker. That night, I felt as if my life was ending, and God wouldn't even have a chance to save me this time—or so I thought! The conversations in my mind were taking over! With the Bible clinched in one arm and the book *Battlefield of the Mind*, by Joyce Meyers, in the other hand, I sat there thinking that no one really loved me. As far as I was concerned, nothing I tried worked or appeared to be true, at least not for me. I finally got tired of fighting the voices in my head. My heart and soul grew weary that night, and I decided it was time to put it all to rest. Oh, how I needed the peace and rest. I was willing to go where I knew it could be found. I had it all figured out this time. I asked God to let me rest, let me come to where He is, and just rest, even if it meant dying. Not remembering that it was a sin, I grabbed the only pills I could put my hands on, which were my blood pressure pills. With my medical background, I knew that if I took the right number of pills, they would reduce my blood pressure so low that it would shut down my heart, my kidneys, and my lungs, and finally I would be resting so peacefully in the arms of God. Needless to say, *things didn't turn out quite the way I planned!*

A CHANGE OF PLANS

I couldn't even get this right! I woke up later in the very same spot, but in a puddle of my own body fluids. First thing I thought was, "Man, God doesn't even want me!" And immediately, the most loving words I could ever hear came gently back to me saying, *"I gave you what you asked for. I gave you rest."* His words to me showed me a deeper side of His care for me that didn't require me to die to rest. This is why in our daily prayer and meditation time, we need to be very specific as to what we want from God. He truly listens to us even though He has His own way of delivering what we ask for. I asked for rest in his arms, and so He did just that.

I dare say that for three days I lay there stretched out in a mess, but in complete rest, with His loving arms holding back the billows of death. He gave me back my life and showed me that He wasn't finished with me. Because my work here was not done, I had to get busy doing it, and this wasn't even about me. He refused to let me take the easy way out. He knew what was in me and how He had prepared me through the various storms I had endured in the past. *Again, things didn't turn out quite the way I planned, and girl, am I glad about it!*

LESSONS FROM THE HEART

It took me a few hours to get myself together, and even then, I was too embarrassed to call anyone. Therefore, I got dressed and drove myself to Urgent Care to make sure I was really ok, that I was really alive. The doctor in the hospital told me that because I had taken such good care of my heart over the years, it essentially kept me going when I had given up. My body took over when my mind had let go.

Beyond my faith in God, eating well, investing in my body, moving, sleeping well, and breathing well helped to save my life. I was trying to shut everything down, but because of all the years I had taken care of myself, my heart found reasons to live on without asking me. My body gave itself *permission to win* for three days while my heart and organs functioned at such a very low rate. They weren't ready to die, and they were willing to do the work for me. Who would think that after all the heartaches and disappointment and all the years I put into building my body that something would work out in my favor. In that moment, my faith was renewed like the eagle, and I walked away knowing three things for sure:

1) *God really does love me.* Never question your faith or His love for you. It expands farther than the eye can see and deeper than the heart can comprehend. Because of His love, you can walk through anything, knowing that you can win in this thing called life.

2) *I now know how to be a friend.* I laid there, three whole days and no one, not even a girlfriend, came to see about be. I blamed people for my situations and pushed them away, and when I needed them most, they weren't there. It was my chilling reality, but it's your warning. Learn to be a good friend, stay close, and never push good people away in your life. Check in on the people you love, and don't let time go by without letting them know you love them and care about them.

3) *What I do does matter.* We are responsible for our actions, but we are not in control of the consequences. Be careful about the choices you make, especially in a time of anger or disappointment. You can take your planned course of action, but you have no way of controlling what will happen as a result of it. Your consequences and rewards are a choice away ... Choose wisely!

Right then and there, I had an "aha moment," and you will have your aha moments, too. I hope yours certainly will come in a different way than mine came. Nevertheless, you will have them, because God loves you, and He knows what you go through each day.

THE FINAL SAY

Things may not turn out quite the way you plan, but at any given moment you have the authority to say, "This is not how my story ends." You have the power to change your perception from one of pain to one of pleasure. You have to learn how to define your situation in a way that empowers you instead of overwhelming you. I did what I knew for sure, and that was to turn it over to God. You, now have to make yourself a priority and turn your challenges over to Him. You have to make the decision to do better for yourself by taking care of your mind, body, and spirit.

For a split second, I truly didn't love myself, but years ago, I made the decision to eat well, be healed from cancer, let go of people and things that were bringing me down, move well, sleep well, and breathe well. This is the formula for living well, because I'm alive today.

Now I travel around the country speaking and teaching men, women, and children how to breathe, how to eat, how to move, and how to engage the elements around them to "Think Well Be Well." I help them synchronize in each aspect of their lives with a goal of achieving their own ultimate state of total wellness. As the owner and operator of Pure Nuphoria Wellness Center, I work with commercial and corporate clients, one-on-one or in groups. In addition to fitness training, I also provide consulting on meal planning and altering lifestyle behaviors.

Through it all, the good and the bad, you can discover your own success. I hope and pray that you understand that wellness is a state of mind. It's not something you do; it's who you become. When life happens, you can depend on your faith and your body's equity to stand up for you in your moments of weakness. Remember that you are not being tested to show your weaknesses, but to discover your strengths and your power. Have a love affair with yourself; fall in love with the process of discovering and building you each day. The power is your hands. You get to decide to Think Well Be Well Now. Give yourself permission ... *And Win Big!*

IT TAKES
TWO

By Susan L. Kee

Daughters of Legacy, Winning in Relationships
Founder, Real Women Real Talk Roundtable
Talk Show Host, "RWRTLive on Me, God and a Cup of Coffee"
SILC—Systematically Influencing Leadership and Change

The challenge will always be *who you are* and *who you want to be*. Who you are is a reflection of your choices, while who you want to be is what you tell yourself when you are alone but often are afraid to express. To win in your relationships, you must consciously choose to allow *who you want to be* to be *who you are*. The two must become one. Who you want to be will be dictated by what you ultimately accept as your core values. Travel with me for just a moment as I show you how to win in every relationship you will encounter in life. *Winning is a choice.*

INTENTIONAL LIVING

Have you ever wondered why some relationships fail? I used to. In fact, if you were to be honest, you would probably say many disappointments have come as a result of failing relationships. I want to talk to you about how to win in your relationships by loving, living, and relating on purpose. It is a skill. Most people spend more time deciding what they will eat than how to have a successful relationship. Unfortunately, we take for granted that once the relationship is established, everything else just falls into place.

With our focus on so many other things that matter, it can be tough to think of every step being done on purpose, even down to how we say hello to one another. From how we communicate in relationships to how we spend our money requires planning and commitment. I have been practicing this idea for some time, and though at times it contradicts everything I thought I knew, I truly know now that living on purpose simplifies one's life.

We build up our belief systems over time. Making decisions to connect with those who don't necessarily look like you or think like you so you can win in a relationship can be challenging, especially if you've always believed that relationships are about what you need and want, and what you will get out of it. It's also normal for us to struggle with trusting new relationships after we've had issues with trust in previous ones.

I love talking about giving yourself *permission to win* in relationships, because to do so you have to know your purpose. We are personally responsible for the outcomes of our relationships. Rick Warren, author of *Purpose-Driven Life*, said, *"Without a purpose, life is motion without meaning, activity without direction, and events without reason. Without a purpose life is trivial, petty, and pointless."* Michael Jackson said, *"I'm looking at the man in the mirror."* Who and what are you looking at for success?

EXPECTATION

Several factors dictate the outcome of your relationships. These factors, while the list is not complete, are important in establishing and understanding real, successful relationships.

First on the list is *Expectation*. A scripture written by the Prophet Jeremiah says, *"For I know the thoughts that I think toward you ... to give you an expected end."* The book of Jeremiah is a message to Judah that warns the people of their outcome if they don't repent. The context of this particular Scripture speaks of the plan of God for a nation after its people had been exiled for 70 years. Often, I take a Scripture and place myself in it. I do this to realize on a greater level my responsibility to others. In other words, when I apply this particular passage to my relationships, it reminds me that no matter what the relationship goes through and however long it may be, the end result should be that the relationship was intentional, or on purpose, even planned. Time and again we quit before we have an opportunity to experience the result or the end. All relationships go through a period of struggle or strain, so that's not an issue. Although we get the urge to quit or give up on the relationship during this period, in order to stay in it, we have to know why we agreed to be in the relationship in the first place and what we devoted to it. This is the expectation of the relationship or friendship.

Expectation can be viewed several ways: What you expect out of the relationship and what you are looking for from the person in the relationship. Though, more important than all of this, I believe, is what a person can expect from *you* in the relationship.

Did you know that others have a right to expect something from you in a friendship? How often have you committed more to a relationship than what you actually had to give? And, how often have we wanted more out of a relationship than a person's ability to give it? When we are honest about what we bring to the relationship as well as what the other person can give us, and we can accept both, then we have an action plan to win. This is because when a person gives genuinely, we can expect not to be disappointed. Being honest about what you bring to the relationship is what enables a person to know what to expect, and the relationship is less likely to fail.

Also, when you are honest about who you are and your capacity to give, it helps you to live up to what you are gifted to give. For example, if you know your friend does not enjoy going to the library for hours at a time, don't expect her to spend endless hours with you in the library. On occasions, an unselfish friend will agree to the trip simply because she, too, cares about what you want. However, to win, don't be disappointed if she doesn't, and moreover, *don't expect it.* I know, you're saying to yourself right now, "This is simple," but so often this is where we lose in relationships. We expect what cannot be given. I fully suggest that you practice early in life accepting people where they are. Besides, don't we want people to accept us where we are?

SACRIFICE AND FORGIVENESS

An important part of winning in relationships is *Sacrifice* and *Forgiveness*. Sacrifice is something you give up for a better cause. Forgiveness is intentionally letting go of negative feelings and the desire for revenge. *"We can forgive a person that has not made a sacrifice, but we cannot forgive without a sacrifice."* I read this quote somewhere and wholeheartedly believe it. In fact, being able to forgive someone after they have disappointed us generally requires sacrificing our feelings, our expectations, and more. Shasta Nelson, author of one of my favorite books, *Friendships Don't Just Happen!* says that *"our ability to repeatedly forgive will not only determine our relational health, but also our personal health."*

I believe that being willing to sacrifice and forgive is the act of giving yourself *permission to win*. Believe it or not, we are hardwired to strike back when we have been hurt. Our feelings and pride are injured. Also, our hopes are disappointed, because generally, we are self-centered. Demanding others to explain their actions is usually greater than our desire to understand their actions. In other words, we generally require an explanation or answer before we simply decide to forgive someone for hurting us. When our desire to understand is greater than our desire to get answers, that is when we have willfully sacrificed, or foregone, our feelings in order to forgive and move on. Forgiveness is ultimately about our own hearts.

Generally, the root of an unhealthy relationship is fear. How you respond in times that call for sacrifice, forgiveness, or expectation has everything to do with how much you love or how much you fear. I am reminded daily that faultless love diminishes fear. When we love others for who they are, they are not afraid to love us back. This does not mean you allow people to treat you badly. It means you don't require from people what you know they cannot give, as I discussed earlier. This is why having more than one friend is good. No one person can ever fulfill every area of our lives. Only God can do that.

LOVE AND CORE VALUES

No relationship succeeds without *Love*. Love allows you to speak up in a relationship when it is not meeting your expectations and allows others the freedom to speak up. As I previously shared, love gives you the ability to sacrifice and forgive when necessary. The dictionary describes love as a deep affection for someone or something. I believe this, love will give and take (sacrifice) time, energy, or even space to uphold a friendship.

Love will never compromise its core values, but first you have to know what your core values are. Do you know what your core values are? They are the principles that dictate your behavior and actions, or the things that help you to know right from wrong. Your core values shape what you are willing to sacrifice. Take a few minutes and list your core values. This will become the basis by which you build your relationships.

To be committed to a friendship or relationship, you must know your core values, and you must know that the other person respects them. If a person does not respect your core values, your relationship is destined to fail. Loving someone unconditionally is one thing that does not require anything on your part except the decision to love. However, spending time with someone that does not respect your core values requires you to accept less for yourself, and that is not what this is about. Never accept less for yourself. You have a right to expect great things in your life.

FACING CONFLICT

While relationships are to be taken seriously, they are still about winning and losing. The choice is yours. Giving yourself *permission to win* means being willing to face conflict head on and not quitting when you are challenged to stretch beyond what you know about yourself. Effective, healthy relationships will always endure conflict. Conflicts of needs, wants, preferences, interests, opinions, beliefs, and values are all part of winning in relationships. In the end, winning in relationships requires unconditional love, and love is unconditional when it endures despite unfavorable circumstances. Have you given yourself *permission to win?*

Sometime ago, I made a conscious decision to give myself *permission to win* in my relationships. Believe me, it was not easy. First, I had to stop blaming others for my hurt. I chose to be hurt. I know you may have a hard time believing that, but you get to define the experience for yourself. Have you ever wondered why we are often hurt by those we love? It's because they can get the closest to our hearts. Truth is, we are often shocked and feel "hurt" when those we love disappoint us. Nevertheless, it is how we handle disappointments and what we choose to do with the information that make the difference. We can forgive, we can walk away, we can forgive and walk away, or we can forgive and stay. The choice is ours.

Though I've heard it many times, I ultimately had to realize that hurting people hurt people. That being said, I just decided to be love with the goal of loving the hurt away. In other words, we must be kind to people when they don't expect it. When I made this decision, my life took a turn. No longer was I a victim of others who disappointed me. I became champion in my own life. By choosing to love and to allow love to happen, failing in relationships is not an option. By actively seeking what I can give versus what I can get, I am never disappointed. It's true that love is reciprocal, and we should expect to get back what we put in. Just remember, you are just learning this lesson, so this will put you ahead of the game. Others may not understand this yet.

THE ULTIMATE CHOICE

I will never cease to be a person who loves no matter what, because I am love. When I intentionally choose to love, love is always present. Winning in relationships can be difficult if your expectations are not met. So, why not make up your mind today to be a winner in your friendships, in your relationships, and in your community. Make the following confession every day: *"I choose to love. I choose to win. I choose to connect. I choose to be a part. I choose to sacrifice. I choose to forgive."*

These are just some of the choices that you will have to make to develop strong relationships. Decide to be actively responsible for the outcome of your relationships. Yes, it will take work. All great things do. Give yourself *permission to win* in your relationships; your life will never be the same.

BY ANY MEANS
NECESSARY

By Pamela A. Williams

Daughters of Legacy, Winning in Business
Program Director, Muhammad Ali Childhood Home Museum
Owner/CEO, CorpEx Intl
Founder, The Pink Connection Mentoring
Sales Director, Mary Kay Cosmetics
Co-Author, *My Now, The Student Leader*

Growing up in Louisville, Kentucky, was challenging, exciting, hopeful, and rewarding, and brought about many life lessons for a young African-American girl. My parents were very loving, positive, and supportive. They taught my younger brother and I to seek always to be the best, be different, be proud of who we were, and, most importantly, never settle for less or let anyone make us feel less than a person. I grew up in the mid to late 1970s as a teenager and at a time when desegregation started in the Jefferson County School System. By the time I graduated from high school, I had attended five different schools between grades six and twelve, when most students may have only experienced enrollment in two schools during those years. Attending different schools was instrumental in affording me the opportunity to meet new people, learn different cultures, and establish new friends along every step of the way.

CLASS IS IN SESSION

In the late 1970s when the Jefferson County School System was desegregated in Louisville, desegregation wasn't widely accepted by other races. Many of us students didn't know what to expect, nor were we prepared for the actions of others. I vividly recall the National Guard escorting us to school and being on our bus to ensure we weren't hurt by protesters or White students who made many threats. They would throw things at our bus; they called us the "N" word and told us not to come back to "their" school.

Those troubling years, primarily my sixth and seventh grade school years, were so long ago, yet I remember them like they happened yesterday. Was I scared? Of course. Did it make me not want to go back to those schools? Of course. Yet, my classmates and I persevered, and we survived. In fact, we thrived! We were leaders and had a voice in our school. Lyrics in one of Katy Perry's songs say, *"What doesn't kill you makes you stronger."* These few words were certainly what I lived by back then. I was never hurt physically, but I was challenged emotionally/mentally, and those challenges helped to mold my character into who I am today—a strong woman and mother.

In junior and senior high school, I participated in track, cross-country, and basketball. Being idle wasn't an option; I was always into things, stayed busy, and loved being around people. And it didn't stop; I was the same way in college, always volunteering and participating in campus activities. As a freshman in college, I pledged the Alpha Kappa Alpha Sorority, Inc., because I was drawn to the sister connection. But it wasn't just the sister connection; it was also very important for me to be involved in an organization that supported women's causes, the community, and humanitarian and philanthropic efforts. Not having any sisters growing up, the sorority life really appealed to me, and I met some phenomenal women, whom I'm still very close to today.

THE DARKER THE BERRY

In the late '60s and '70s, being dark-skinned wasn't favorable for me. Thank God, I had a mother and father who taught me that no matter the color of my skin, I was beautiful. The unfortunate part was that most of society didn't have the same view. People made comments about my skin tone, even throughout my college years. I would hear comments such as, "She's a pretty *dark-skinned* girl." Really! Why couldn't I just be pretty? I used to ask myself that question a lot. Because I had high self-esteem and was proud of who I was, I was able to look past those comments and maintain who I was and who I would become in life as a woman.

Along with the skin-color craziness came the skinny comments. Yes, my legs were like sticks. So, what! Yes, I was called "Knobby Knees." So, what! Maybe you've been called such names, or maybe worse. Again, I truly lived by the adage, "Sticks and stones may break my bones, but words will *never* hurt me." I had to ignore the ignorance and pettiness that were so common during those times.

BALANCING ACT

My dad was instrumental in my childhood, always teaching us African-American history in order to preserve our rich culture. I was introduced to the Black Pride movement early in life. I would always accompany my dad to hear the Reverend Jesse Jackson, Angela Davis, and many others speak. Hearing those speakers gave me a huge sense of self-love, a love for who I was and for my skin color, and an appreciation for the struggles our people endured so we are now able to have some of the rights and privileges we have today.

As a result of the struggle and the constant affirmation from those that loved me, I continued to develop a strong self-image and had high self-esteem. The only thing that bothered me was the ignorance of other people. Often, if someone made the remark about my skin tone, I would respond that "Black is beautiful!" Or when they remarked that I was a "pretty *dark-skinned* girl," I would say, "Yes, I am!" My prayers are that our society, particularly in the African-American community, continues to move beyond this mindset. I'd like to think we have; however, there remain some detractors. We are beautiful in any shade, color, or size!

ON MY OWN

In 1988, a few years after graduating from college, I decided to relocate to Silver Spring, Maryland, a suburb of Washington, DC I packed up my small Toyota Corolla and hit the road headed for Maryland. This was a huge step, because I didn't have a job, only a small savings, and had no place to live (I had to live with friends for a few months). The one thing I had was *Faith*. I knew that no matter what, I would find a way to make a way. My parents had taught me to be resourceful.

Those first few years away from home allowed me to grow as a woman and grow professionally. By making that huge leap of faith, I met some phenomenal people in the Washington, DC, area who helped me along the way. Throughout my many years of living in the DC area, I made tremendous inroads within the community. I started volunteering with a local English for Speakers of Other Languages (ESOL) program, teaching foreign students how to read English. From there I got involved with church groups and other local activities that focused on helping people, or women and children in particular. The one thing I have always been passionate about is being able to give back and teach.

For many years, I wanted to start a business or organize a mentoring group for young women. It was in these crucial years of my life, between the ages of 25 to 30, that I felt the transition, or shift, begin to happen. What I noticed in the DC area was that so many African-American women and men owned their own businesses. So here I was, a young woman from Louisville, attempting to leave my footprint in the DC area where so many others were trying to do the same thing. I asked myself many questions: "How would I do it?" "Would I be accepted?" "What makes me different from others?" "What do I have to offer?" These questions just went on and on and on in my mind.

When you want something to happen, you have to just jump right in with both feet. I strived to learn as much as I could about owning and running a business.

NEVER ALONE

Let's fast-forward another 12 years. By this time, I had earned my master's degree in Human Resources Management. In 1996, I landed a position with a staffing agency in DC and met a super woman by the name of Myrna Cooks. Under the 22-year tutelage of Ms. Cooks, my professional career developed, and she remains one of my mentors today.

Under her mentorship, I learned so much. She helped me develop my leadership skills, hone my professional speaking skills, develop a general business acumen, and run a business successfully. She also taught me general life skills, such as to be true to self, that my word is my bond, to never give up, to believe in myself, and the list goes on and on. She really was a *super woman!*

As a result of having a great mentor and wonderful, supportive, and encouraging parents, life has been good to me. I've never had any difficulty taking advantage of great career opportunities. I worked in corporate America for 27 years and retired in 2013; those years were great. The time I spent growing as a professional, increasing my knowledge, mastering certain skills, and soaking in as much knowledge as I could prepared me to take a leap of faith to leave corporate America and start my own business.

WORTH IT ALL

I stand proud of all of my accomplishments. I have had a very successful professional career and have been able to partner and collaborate with exceptional women and men on many social, economic, and community efforts.

Currently, I'm proud to hold the position as the Program Director of the newly opened Muhammad Ali Childhood Home Museum in Louisville. This appointment was not in my plans, but God prepared me for it. I stepped into a brand-new role, and I had to get it done—*everything!* But guess what. I wasn't scared. You see, I was well-prepared for that moment. This was the result of the former 33 years of hard work, dedication, commitment, and servanthood.

NOW IT'S YOUR TURN

My word for you today is *Empowered.* When you're empowered, you can take on the world. Feeling empowered gives you *permission to win!* Not only do I empower myself, but I also look forward each day to empowering others. My legacy will be that I committed my life to serving others. I'm committed to continue to fortify my legacy with servant-hood, always giving to others whether it is of my time, my talents, my knowledge, or my finances.

What can you do right now? I recommend that you find a mentor, if you don't already have one. This is someone who will challenge you to reach higher heights, stretch your mind far beyond where you ever imagined, and encourage you along the way.

Give yourself *permission to win* by speaking positivity over your life. Start each day with the affirmation, *"Today I will be better than yesterday."* Make up your own affirmations, and say them daily. Keep a positive mind, never speaking negativity. I believe in the power of our words. I recommend you read Joel Osteen's book, *The Power of I Am.* In addition, I strongly believe in a Mary Kay Ash's quote *"God didn't make a nobody, only a somebody ...."* And that somebody is you.

Finally, follow your dreams, and don't give up. Nothing worth fighting for will be easy, so don't stop fighting. Give yourself *permission to win* by any means necessary!

INCREDIBLY
AWESOME

By Maria Stanfield

Daughters of Legacy, Winning the Workplace
Founder and CEO, My Sister's Closet and MSC Career
Consulting Services

Career Acceleration Coach, Catalyst for Change,
Motivation Speaker and Professional Development Youth
Instructor
Profiled in the *Washington Business Journal*, Change at
the Top: a Two-Part Series About Making the Most of
Management Changes
2016 Panelist Speaker, Steve Harvey, Act Like a Success
Conference; 2016 AVP President's Award Winner;
2013 Kingdom Living

I was out enjoying a beautiful, autumn day with a good girlfriend of mine, who's also one of my mentors, when a gentleman passerby's comment sparked a laughing fest. The simple comment was, "Girl, you look like money." I replied, "If you only knew." We laughed until we cried!

You see, far too often we look at a person and figure we know her whole life story. Has that ever happened to you? Maybe someone said to you, "I thought you were this." Or "I thought you were that." It happens all the time. So, when the gentleman said, "You look like money," I just couldn't hold back the laughter.

I AM NOT MY STORY

I may in fact look like money today, with my designer clothes and shoes, but let me tell you that's not where I started. Yes, today, I am the Founder, Owner, and CEO of two successful companies; a non-profit organization, My Sisters Closet; and a for-profit business, MSC Career Consulting Services. Yes, I also work for a prestigious law firm as an Office Administrator (no, I'm not a lawyer, yet my corner office is the size of a small apartment, and I make a generous six-figure salary). Impressed? Well, many people would be, but that's only part of the story. What's really interesting is that I did it all with only a high-school education, and truthfully, I barely made it out of high school with a D average.

As a little girl, I was teased a lot, and I mean a lot! People told me that I was too skinny, and, at six feet tall in the ninth grade, that I was too tall. They also said that I was too stupid, that I couldn't write or type as well as the others, and that the only grade I would ever get would be a D because D stood for Dumb. The worst of part of it all was I started to believe them. And sadly, I let that hold me back for a very long time. Words have power, so watch what you say even when you are joking. You'll have whatsoever you say.

BUT GOD ...!

Thinking back, little did they know where I'd be today. In fact, as I think back when I was a young girl, I didn't know or believe that I'd be as successful as I am today. I'm grateful that God allowed me to turn lemons into lemonade. They didn't know that tall, skinny, dark-skinned girl would take the sticks and stones they threw at her and create stepping stones to launch a career as a fashion model at age 19. They didn't know that the storms that raged in my life were watering my hopes and dreams. They didn't know that God had planted seeds of success inside me long before I knew how to write my name. So, every time they gossiped about me and threw dirt on me, they were in fact fertilizing my potential and helping me to grow into the woman I am today.

DIVINE APPOINTMENTS

You must understand that my transformation didn't happen overnight. It took time, and God is still working on me. Starting with my mother and grandmothers, God placed some incredible role models and mentors in my life who were divinely assigned to me to counteract some of the ugly things people said to me and about me. These beautiful women constantly reminded me of who I was, and they believed in me; yet I still struggled with insecurity. Mommy, Daddy and grand-mommies *have* to love you, but what about the rest of the world. Right?

After my on-and-off modeling career, I started working at a major law firm in Washington, DC, and this is where the metamorphosis of my life truly began. Surrounded by powerful women in a predominately male industry, I was inspired, empowered, and mentored by the best. I learned four particularly powerful steps that I believe every young lady needs to implement in her life while she's on the road to success. I like to call then, Maria's Mentoring Moments.

IRON SHARPENS IRON

The first thing I would like for you to do is to find a mentor. Seek out a positive role model whom you trust, someone who has your best interest at heart, not theirs, and not what's in it for them. My first mentor was my boss, and she told me the cold, hard truth, even if it hurt my feelings or made me feel bad in the moment. I had to realize that she was telling me these things because she cared about me and wanted the best for me. One example was about my work clothes. Remember, I told you I was a model? So, my clothes were not the standard "office attire." She told me to dress in more professional suits, dresses, etc., so I shopped yard sales and thrift stores before they were considered "cool," like they are now. It cost me more to get clothes dry-cleaned than what I paid for them, but it worked. I learned to dress sharp every day, because I saw my mentor and other sharp women I admired looking professional. (Funny, I don't think that passerby would have said I looked like money back then when I smelled like a hint of math balls. Do you? But again, he didn't know my story or my real struggle.)

HEADS UP

Secondly, you must have a winning attitude. Did you know that you get to choose your attitude every day? A positive attitude can do wonders for you. It will reduce negative emotions; attract people to you; and give you favor with teachers, professors, and supervisors. For example, have you ever been around people with horrible attitudes? No matter what the conversation is about, they have something negative to say. Something is always wrong with this, that, and other people. How do they make you feel? Personally, I just want to get away from them. How about you?

Negativity brings you down, and misery loves company, so take my advice and stay positive. Even when on some days you don't feel as good as you feel on other days, put on a positive attitude just like you put on your clothes each day. Use that same power to put on thoughts of success, prosperity, joy, and love. That will bring out a winning attitude that will help you with your self-esteem and how you feel about yourself. With so much negativity in the world, it's important that you think well of yourself. I have found in my life that when I am positive about myself, other people around me will have a better opinion of me also. Having a positive attitude is intentional; you have to think positive to be positive. When you think positive, you enhance your confidence, courage, inner strength, and beauty.

MIRROR! MIRROR!

Thirdly, you must tighten your image. Your image is what people think of you. It's your Gucci, your Chanel, your own personal brand. What do your clothes and hair say about you? Do people say you are trendy, fashionable, expensive, cheap, or thrifty? Just as the passerby commented, he made an assumption in just a few seconds on what he saw. He told himself a story without my saying one word. Wow! Imagine that! It happens all the time, and we all do the same thing every day; so, consider that how you dress really does matter. You may never hear what people say about you, so make sure your image is reflecting what you intend for it to say.

HAVE FAITH

Finally, you must have faith. Faith is defined as confidence in what we hope for and the assurance about what we do not see. I didn't know what I wanted to do when I grew up, but I knew I wanted to be important, have nice things, and be an inspiring speaker. I would sit and stare at people who had all those qualities and the things I desired and long to be just like them. Yet it seemed unreachable, because I was so insecure, and all the negative things that had been said about me I still believed. Then one day, I read the truth about myself in the Bible. It says that I *am fearfully and wonderfully made.* "Wonderfully," I understood, but "fearfully" ... What did that mean?

I looked up the meaning of "fearfully" to understand fully what the Bible was trying to tell me. The word "fearfully" in the Bible means in awe of, reverence, extreme, and intense. I hung on that first part, *in awe of.* That's what I thought of other "successful looking" people when I looked at them; I was in awe of them. And the Bible says this same thing about me, too! I am Awe-some, too! I just needed to have faith and believe it for myself. I did just that! I wonder if that's what the passerby saw in me ... my awesomeness!

LIVE YOUR AWESOMENESS

Now I realize the passerby didn't see my struggles. He never saw the little girl or even the adult who struggled with confidence. He didn't see me working long, hard hours when everyone else had gone home, or when I was trying to figure out basic math problems so I wouldn't embarrass myself the next day. He never knew I was in the bathroom crying from exhaustion after being up all night with two sick kids and working a 10-hour workday, then going home to do it all over again. He didn't feel the hurtful words that people said to me year after year. He never saw any of that. He simply saw what God had done in my life. He saw God's *awesomeness* in me.

That same *awesomeness* is in you. You have to remember who you are and whose you are. And if you don't know who you are the way I didn't know at one time, then I invite you to read the Bible and ask God to show you who you are. One thing for sure is that He said you are *awesome* and *wonderful*, and the seeds of success are planted in you and getting watered every day through the showers and the storms of life. Be patient with yourself, be confident in who you are, and live in your awesomeness!
Be blessed, little sister!

HEAD OF
THE CLASS

By Cassandra W. Dickerson

Daughters of Legacy, Winning in Education
Professor, Morgan State University
PhD Student, Iowa State University
Author, *Well Done!*
Co-Founder, Artelia Williams Educational Scholarship

Growing up, I must confess that I was one of the kids who loved school. I always had perfect attendance, primarily because I went to school even when I was sick. I wouldn't advise doing that nowadays, but that's how we did it back then. In fact, something had to be really wrong for me to miss school. I now realize I was so committed to school because I truly loved to learn.

It's no mistake or coincidence that I am now an educator at Morgan State University and working toward my PhD in Apparel, Merchandising and Design from Iowa State University. In addition to my love for reading and writing, with English being my favorite subject, I also loved spelling, foreign language, and many other subjects. Truthfully, I just really loved the school atmosphere: it was a place where I received new information; embarked upon challenging quests; and related to wonderful teachers, classmates, and friends.

In hindsight, I can see how competitive I was and probably still am today. Being very athletic, I played sports and ran track. In grade school, I was the second fastest runner in my class. I really thought I was the fastest, but when a girl from another class raced against me, I would surely come in second place.

WHAT DOESN'T BREAK YOU ...

Although I was very popular in school, always friendly and very outgoing, I still faced some challenges. A person or two may have disliked me, or treated me badly, but that goes with the territory. As I think back on it, one main bully was in our class. She chose a person each week whom she didn't like and told everyone else not to be that person's friend! Wow! Can you believe it? And to think, some people actually listened to her. Bullying is still common today, so know who you are, and always let someone know if a person is bullying you. After all, the bully is the one with the problem!

Some of my other challenges were that I didn't always have the money I wanted or needed, and I had to wear less than the latest and greatest designer clothing and accessories. That didn't stop a thing, though. My mother, Artelia Williams, was a strong, confident woman who instilled that same confidence in each of her children. Because of her, I always had a sense of who I am and that I could achieve whatever I set out to do. As a result, I made my own couture clothing and eventually traveled across the globe to study textiles and manufacturing in Hong Kong, China. Now I teach it on the collegiate level. It's also because of my mother, an educator herself, that I am committed to equipping my students to excel beyond their limitations and use all their God-given talents to the fullest. Try to remember that others see your potential even if you don't!

AUTHENTICALLY ME

As I look back over my life, I can see how it all—the good and the not so good—played a major role in who I am today. Because of my experiences, I discovered the power of being my authentic self. Each day, I set out to be *authentically me*, because it's what holds true for me. Over the years, I've also discovered what I value, the things that are important to me. Being *authentically me* means proactively living those values out on a daily basis. This includes basing my decisions, in every area of my life, on these values. This is not always easy, and I didn't always do this; but once I realized it, the core of my being began to flourish. I not only understood what was important to me, but I also realized what was important to God. Now, I work everything in life through the grid of my values, then I set out to do and to be that person more and more. Living based on core values is extremely important, no matter what your vocation, profession, or goals are in life. I have found that it is a fundamental principle that supports me in any area or facet of life. It is what makes me true to myself first, and then I can be true to others.

SELF-ACTUALIZE

Though similar to identity and knowing who you are, self-actualization is much deeper. It goes even farther beyond the so important "must" of knowing who you are and why you are here. If one bases self-actualization on Maslow's Hierarchy of Needs, then self-actualization can be thought of as a point when one moves beyond basic human needs—survival, physical needs, security, safety, and even love. It's past the need to belong. It's when you esteem *you*. It's self-esteem—the need to feel competent, confident, and strong; and the need to feel able, valuable, and worthwhile. It's when I realize that my need to feel this way is ok, that I am those things—competent, confident, and strong. I am able, valuable, and worthwhile, because I belong to God and because He made me. Then I'm able to self-actualize. When I self-actualize, I realize my full potential and function at full capacity.

Again, this is by no means an easy journey. It took a while for me to get here, and even now I vacillate back and forth from time to time. This is what makes *permission to win* possible. I realize now that feeling the opposite of those things (unworthy, unimportant, weak, or unsure) was ok, because it took me feeling those things first to know (hint: *actualize*) or come into realization that I am more than that. It's feeling those things and sitting in them—giving myself permission to feel and experience them. Then it's permission to move beyond them—to tell myself I am who God says I am—that gives me *permission to win.*

The same goes for you. Don't be afraid to feel and assess those thoughts of inadequacies, but don't stay there. Once you are fully aware of what it's trying to speak to you, at that moment you have the power to override it with what God says about you. Receiving this truth as your own gives you *permission to win.*

WINNING COMBINATION

I love the quote *"to thine own self be true."* When you're true to yourself, you allow yourself to see *you*—your behaviors, attitudes, character—and it's not always pretty. No indeed! So, when you *permit* yourself to acknowledge that all those things are who you are *being*, then you can believe that God, the universe, and you all come into agreement and alignment for change and new possibilities for your life. It is then that you can truly start functioning to full capacity. It is then that your *"soul can prosper."* Then you can be your highest and greatest self, and give the highest and greatest good to others in every situation, in every scenario, and everywhere you go. You become the manifestation of an unseen God. This is how you and I give ourselves *permission to win.*

It's a known fact that when you write things down, you are more likely to accomplish them. Try writing down the following three strategies, and keep them in a safe place as a daily reminder. These strategies have helped me and continue to help me give myself *permission to win:*

1) *Like yourself.* Self-identity is very important. Once you know *you*, and more importantly accept *you*, others will do the same. Spend more and more time each day getting to know, love, and appreciate the *you* who you are.

2) *Do what you love.* Find what you are passionate about, and you will succeed. People are waiting for what you will bring to the world, and your passion will keep you going for it!

3) *Remember your Creator.* There is absolutely *no way* I could have accomplished anything that I have done without my God. My faith and relationship with God are of upmost importance to me. Establish a relationship with God, and allow Him to give you purpose. Then you can live your life fulfilling His supreme purpose for your life.

As a simple reminder, never stop learning. The classroom is not the only place you can learn. What you are looking for is looking for you. Ask, seek, and knock, and the universe will be opened to you.

SECTION TWO:
WINNING STRATEGIES
FROM SUCCESSFUL

POWER
PLAYERS

PERMISSION TO WIN

TOPICS OF INTEREST

Looking for something special?
Read about specific subjects on these pages.

PART ONE:

DISCOVER
THE WINNER WITHIN

"Champions keep playing until they get it right."
~Billie Jean King

WORTH IT
ALL

-By Elder Bernadette Ellis Harris-

Entrepreneur and Business Owner
27 Years as Senior Manager with McDonald's
(Corporate and Private)
Leadership Development for Managers

How the world judges worth is not what matters. Society judges it by popularity, wealth, looks, fashion, size and weight, sexual prowess, and the like. Don't get wrapped up in all that. Fashions change, trends change, people change, and what is deemed acceptable changes. What's constant is what God thinks about you. You are worth far more than rubies, because His Word tells you that. It says that you are the apple of His eye. You are a prized possession who is worth Christ's sacrifice. Now, it's up to you to receive it, believe it, and walk confidently in it. Yes, I know; He sees all the mistakes you have made and the things you would like to improve. However, first and foremost, He sees you as His own. You are royalty, forgiven, beautiful, peculiar, the head, above, victorious, and set apart for His unique purpose; and most of all, you are loved.

So, start loving yourself each day. Concentrate on what's right instead of what's not quite right. If you don't like something about yourself, fix it, because you should and because you can. Carry yourself in a manner that makes you proud of who you are. Take the time to write affirmations that remind you of who you are, and rehearse them daily. Read books and listen to music that affirms your beauty instead of comparing yourself to others. In other words, protect your self-esteem, live in your worth, understand your royal position, and enter into your wealthy place.

LOVE YOU, BE YOU AND HONOR WHO YOU ARE!

By Jennifer L. Hamilton

City-wide Senior Special Events Coordinator
DC State Senior Games Coordinator
Community Activist

When I was growing up, my self-esteem was extremely low, and I sought attention by doing the wrong things. After my father got sick, he sat me down and said:

"You can't do this foolishness anymore. You have to *love* you, *be* you, and *honor* who you are. Ask yourself, 'Do you want to continue to live like this?' Or will you continue to strive to be a greater you? It's *your* choice."

I decided to get it together by taking responsibility for my actions. As a result of my mental shift, I became the Senior Class Speaker at my high school graduation. I did so well that my speech was featured in *The Washington Post*.

Today, I'm a proud member of Electa Chapter #6, Order of the Eastern Star; the National Congress of Black Women, DC Metropolitan Chapter; and the District of Columbia City-Wide Senior Ambassadors.

The one thing I put into place to give myself *permission to win* is to *always* remember to love me, be me, and honor me. This is what I pass on to you. *Love you*, because there is no one like you; *be you*, and be the best you that you can be; and *honor who you are*. It sets the precedence for how others will treat you. Trust and believe; everything else will fall right into place at the right time when you *love, be, and honor you*.

BEAUTY STARTS
WITHIN

By Tamara McKnight

Author, *The Images of Me*
Motivational Speaker
Advocate and Survivor of Sexual Abuse

Throughout the years, I've faced many obstacles and circumstances, the greatest of these being self-love. Growing up not knowing how to love myself was not only my biggest challenge, but also day to day I had to wake up and look into a mirror at a girl who was lost and didn't know if she could be found. Beautiful she was indeed on the outside, but what good was that if she couldn't see the inner beauty for herself. That became my quest, to discover the true essence of who I was from the inside out and to love what was revealed.

The same goes for you. You don't have to change a thing about your outer appearance until you discover the real you and learn to love her. After you nurture your inner beauty, the outside will begin to spring forth. Others will begin to recognize the great love, care, and respect you have for yourself, and they in return will realize they, too, must honor you in the appropriate way. However, it all starts with you. Beauty starts within. God has given me a newfound spirit of self-love that I pray you will also receive. Keep praying, Beautiful One. Be patient, and love yourself first.

DO YOU

– By Dr. Reneé Starlynn Allen –

The People's Emcee, Author, Recording Artist
www.ReneeStarlynnSpeaks.com; www.ListenVisionLive.com
Host, "The Renee Allen and Friends Show" on WLVS
Retired Veteran of the U.S. Navy and U.S. Naval Reserves
Honorary Doctorate, Humans Letters Global Oved Dei
Seminary and University
Who's Who in Black Washington, DC, Woman of Excellence

Until you give yourself *permission to win*, you will be stagnant in whatever *you* dream and hope for! You must realize, craft, and release your star power, and then live in it! Your ownership of your star power is the winning strategy you must learn to master. So, there's no need to look at others to mimic their success or envy their destiny. Your star power is simply enough! I am blessed to have parents, Leith and Charlotte Fraser, who taught me this through their integrity and ongoing love and support.

You have been blessed to live a spectacular life that's all yours to create. Even where you are today, you already have everything *you* need to blaze the trail and do great deeds throughout your journey. Fall forward into the arms of a world that's waiting to welcome you and experience all that you have to offer. This means maintaining a positive attitude, for it will be key to navigating through the highs and lows of your journey.

You must also be diligent to take care of yourself in the process. As you begin to reap the harvest that will surely come as a result of your labor, learn to be disciplined with your money and spending habits. The goal is to have a happy and long-lived life, which requires health plus wealth to make it. Your star power will help get *you* there, but your discipline will keep you there. It is your hidden treasure—your secret weapon to playing and winning big—but you have to first give yourself *permission to win* by doing you and being the best *you* that you can ever be! *Bam Boom Pow Dow!*

BELIEVE IN WHO
YOU ARE NOT... YET!

— *By Valerie Royster* —

Founder and Administrator, Kingdom
Christian Academy
Master's Degree in Education
Executive Award for Innovation and Creativity by
Mother's Care Day Care Center

Facilitator of Grammar Classes at WMATA and MasterLife at Evangel Cathedral

The road may be dark and lonely. There are no visuals or particular directions for you to follow. You may wind up in a place of, "How did I get here?" You thought you were going to _____ and you thought you would be doing _____, but none of what you have done can define who you are.

At the end of the day, who we become is much more than who we believed we could be. For all that you are will be revealed as you are "becoming." Your hope is always that you will accomplish everything you set out to do, but your outcome gives birth to so much more than you could have ever imagined. So, keep walking it out, do it even if you're afraid, give it everything you've got, and simply keep "becoming" more than who you ever believed you could be.

When I was young, I made some unwise choices listening to my peers and trying to fit in. Many family members counted me out, and my high school guidance counselor told me to get a vocation because I would never make it through college.

Well, they were all wrong. I became the founder and administrator of the Kingdom Christian Academy with faith and just six students to start. It has blossomed into a viable place of learning and advocacy for many children. Like me, you will become more than you ever can think of right now. Just keep the faith, trust God's commitment to His investment in you, and never ever stop "becoming!"

YOU ARE
ENOUGH!

By Samira Jones

Author, *Tough Skin, A Journey of Survival and
Persevering Life's Challenges*
Founder, Girlfriends—Discovering Your Strength Network
samirajones.com

Middle school is such a tender experience. It's a point of transition where we begin discovering our independence; our responsibilities for self; and, one other thing, our consciousness of what others may think of us. We tend to base our whole worth on perception and popularity instead of on our own confidence from within ourselves. It's even more challenging if we don't have a supportive family or community to help guide us through the process and affirm our identities.

I am here to tell you that you do not need permission from anyone to be *you*. In fact, you are the "You" on whom we've all been waiting, because you *are* enough right now. What others have to say to that is none of *your* business.

I had to teach my daughter this when she was in the fifth grade. It was important for her to know that it's okay to not fit in. You, too, need to know that it's okay not to fit in. In fact, maybe you are called to be the trendsetter, a trailblazer, or an inspiration for hundreds of other young ladies. If the truth be told, special people like you who are designed to be great and to do great things actually *don't* fit in with the crowd. How can you fit in with the ordinary if you are the extraordinary (extra + ordinary)? Now that you think about it, that's pretty cool. Right?

It's time to be bold. *Be courageous. Have faith. Be inspired!*

GRIT, INDOMITABLE SPIRIT, AND LEADERSHIP
By Ilka V. Chavez

International Best-Selling Author, Success University
for Women in Business Book
Founder and President, Corporate GOLD, LLC
Professional Speaker
Ambassador, Heartrepreneur.com network
Ilka@corporate-gold.com

I grew up believing I could accomplish anything I wanted to in life. In my first year of high school in the U.S. after emigrating from Panama, I realized I wasn't learning at the level to which I was accustomed. I shared my concerns with my counselor, and she recommended I apply for the Secondary Education Through Health (SETH) program. At an early age, I knew I wanted to pursue a career in healthcare, so I applied for the program and was accepted. In my last year of high school, I attended classes at Mount Sinai Hospital in New York, which provided a dual education as well as science-based specialty courses, combined with firsthand experience working at the hospital. I traveled from Brooklyn to Manhattan every day at the crack of dawn to attend this program. It took courage, tenacity, perseverance, and an indomitable spirit—that is, a determined spirit—to accomplish this endeavor.

Leadership requires grit and an indomitable spirit. This allows you to take the lead on your life, knowing your strength comes from within you. You are a leader from where you are right now. It goes hand-in-hand with perseverance, and it will set you apart from the rest. No one can grow your greatness but you! When you feel *you can't*, I encourage you to dig deeper and push yourself beyond your mental and physical capacity. This is the key to running a marathon and finishing the race. People described as having *indomitable spirits* don't need pep talks or protein shakes; their strength truly comes from within them.

YOUR REFLECTION
OF YOU

By Regina Robinson

Inner Confidence Strategist
Educational Coach
International Transformational Speaker
Amazon Best Selling Author
Social Media: ReginaRSpeaks

www.reginarobinsonspeaks.com
www.suited4success.org

I didn't always believe I deserved to be a winner. It wasn't until I realized the only thing holding me back was my belief that I didn't deserve all God had in store for me. My doubts, insecurities, and lack of confidence kept me waiting on the sidelines for everyone else to give me *permission to win*. I realized if I wanted to *win*, it would require me to look at myself in the mirror and do some major reflecting from the inside out. You see, my outer confidence shined brightly; however, my inner confidence was shattered. If I could go back and whisper to my eleven-year-old self, I would declare: "No one can ever stop you in life but *you*. So, grant yourself permission today!" Then I would say: "I am ready, I am destined, and I deserve to be a *winner!*

Oprah Winfrey once said, "Always remember: God can dream a bigger dream than you can ever dream yourself." Dreams are discovered while your eyes are closed, but to make them a reality, you have to open your eyes every day with the determination that achieving your dreams is possible. The reality of your dreams may sometimes seem distant. You may experience setbacks and failures, but remember, they are detours, not stop signs. I promise along your journey you will discover *the winner within you!*

I leave you with this question: What mark will you make on the world?

Everyday declare: "I am *Unbreakable*, I am *Unapologetic*, and I am *Unstoppable!!!*

DISCOVER THE WINNER WITHIN

Affirmation

Today, I am a winner, because the winner lives inside me. I commit to loving, being, and honoring who God created me to be. It is my right to nurture my inner beauty with a positive reflection and a strong belief in who I am becoming. I am the unique expression of the heart of God; therefore, I am enough. I am worth it all. I am unstoppable. I am the head and not the tail, above and not beneath, and the lender and not the borrower. I give myself permission to be a leader, do me, and win big!

PART TWO

POSITION YOURSELF
TO SUCCEED

*"Vision without action is a daydream.
Action without vision is a nightmare."*
~ Japanese proverb

A NAME BRAND
REALITY
By Raven L. Coit

Delaware State University Graduate
Selected for the European Heritage Tour of Six Countries as
a People to People Student Ambassador
Steve Harvey's Disney Dreamers Academy Graduate
Future Graduate Student, Clinical Psychology
National Society of Leadership Success Honoree and

92

PERMISSION TO WIN

National Society of Collegiate Scholar
Clarinetist in the DSU Approaching Storm Marching Band

As young women, we are all winners. Our visions, along with perseverance, can lead our dreams into name brand realities. One strategy that helped me along the way comes from a quote I once heard: "*Sometimes the road to success is through trial and error, but how you prosper in the end will make it all worthwhile.*" When life is not going quite the way I would like, I refer to this quote and remain positive. It always leads me to greater outcomes and achievements than I had originally planned.

When I applied to colleges, I knew attending North Carolina A&T was in my future. However, the Office of Admissions lost my transcripts at least six times. As I waited for North Carolina A&T's response, all of the other letters from colleges arrived. I was disappointed but remained positive, because higher education was in my DNA. Within days of my disappointment, my high school band director approached me and suggested that I audition for Delaware State University's band. After taking his advice, I received an on-the-spot scholarship! Not only did I become a student of another Historically Black College and University, but I also maintained a high grade-point average and was proudly added to the university's Dean's List and President's List each semester. As a result of my perseverance, I am graduating with a B.S. in Psychology a year early. So, it's important for you to stay positive even when things seem to be out of whack. Live out the journey toward your aspirations in a way that produces a one-of-a-kind reality.

CONSISTENCY
IS KEY!

By Leisel L. Taylor

Real Estate Professional in Maryland and DC
One of the Top 20 Producing Members of the
Prince Georges County Association of Realtors
Appeared on Several Television and Radio Shows, including
HGTV's House Hunters, DIY Network, and Fox 5DC
leiseltaylor.yourkwagent.com

I looked at my Wells Fargo checking account balance—$6.31. It was Tuesday, and there would be no paycheck until Friday. My husband's check was a joke. The cable contractor he worked for reduced its cable rates by half, but his check kept the utilities active in the house. I looked at the available credit on my Chase credit card—$43.67—and calculated the baby formula and diaper expenses for my then-8-month-old son—$39.87. I vowed that day was the last time I was going to be in such a situation. Something needed to change immediately. My home was being sold as a short sale, and the realtor who was handling the sale impressed me. This experience began my journey into the real estate world, which has made me disciplined to continue to be successful. I have to do certain tasks *every day* to continue to grow my business. If I don't perform these activities daily, I know I will do an injustice to my family.

Fast-forward 5 years, and I am now one of the Top 20 Realtors in Prince George's County. My husband and I own a successful real estate business, and we can truly say being consistent was a key strategy to our success.

Things must be done regularly to be effective and to be your best. Some days you may feel like giving up, but remember my testimony and how being consistent helped me turn my life around. If you realize that success happens gradually, then suddenly, you won't give up. If you think you want to give up, push through, stay consistent, and pray. It will pay off!

THE POWER
OF GRACE

—By First Lady
Angela R. Gerald—

Co-Founder and First Lady,
Strong Tower Christian Church, Frederick, MD
www.stccfrederick.com

I remember transitioning from middle to high school and then graduation. I was excited and fearful, wondering if I was smart enough or pretty enough, or if I would even fit in with everyone. These feelings can be overwhelming at times, and even today, I find myself sometimes consumed by them. We can be so critical of ourselves and end up putting a lot of pressure on ourselves, when all we really need is the *power of grace.*

Grace requires you to give yourself a break. I had to learn to be confident in who I am, love who God made me to be, and walk proudly in that knowledge. This caused me to change my perspective:

1) I had to acknowledge that I'm not perfect, and I don't have to be—that's the *power of grace.*

2) When I give grace to myself, it's easier to give it to others.

3) For every challenge I endure, I am stronger. I give myself permission to fail, but learning from my failures is a major contributor to my success. Challenges make champions!

You have the power to acknowledge your imperfections, extend grace to yourself and others, and grow through your challenges—all because of the power of grace. I encourage you to give yourself the *power of grace* each day and watch it change your life.

NOTHING BUT
THE BEST

By Keymiah Parmely

Future Pediatrician Surgeon
Honor Roll Student since Pre-Kindergarten
Top Sales Producer
Principal Honor Roll Recipient
Junior Mentor in Jewels One-on-One High Teen Society
Queens 2 Bee Community Queen Ambassador

As an 11-year-old in the sixth grade, I know what it's like to work hard. I attend Howard University Middle School of Mathematics and Science, which makes sure we are grounded in our work habits and lessons. Four things helped me to be successful, besides the fact that I love learning and going to school:

1) *You need a support system.* This can be your family, teachers, and friends, or anyone else who pushes you and makes sure you have what you need to succeed. It's important to show appreciation to them, so try to do something nice for them in order to say "thank you," such as doing what they ask you to do when they ask you to.

2) *You must believe in yourself, and do what you know you can do.* I like trying different things, because I'm not afraid to make a mistake. This also allows you to see what you are good at doing. My mom always encourages me to dream big and listen to my ideas. Then she, along with my family, makes sure I know that I can do anything I put my mind to and that I can make it.

3) *Have pride in yourself.* I like being my best, so I study hard, make sure I look nice when I go out, and do what I know makes my family proud.

4) *Finally, have faith in God.* I pray to God, and it helps me believe in myself. You will need help with your dreams, and He will give you the answers you need when you pray.

In the end, you have to keep encouraging yourself and give yourself permission to be your best.

COMPARTMENTALIZE
TO WIN!

—— By Jacquie Catona Wayans ——

Host and Producer of Don't Give Up and Win
www.jacquiewayans.com

There I was, a 36-year-old, single mother of three middle school children, living in a one-bedroom basement apartment, and attempting to finish my B.A. degree at Columbia University. It wasn't until my marriage fell apart and I became a social pariah that the thought of returning to college became a necessity and not just a wish.

I was on Food Stamps and Medicaid and could barely make ends meet. I had to reduce my work schedule to part-time while still functioning as PTA president and youth leader, and while singing on the choir. I was simultaneously, going through a divorce with no support. It was just Jesus and I.

To succeed, I had to compartmentalize my life. When I was at school, at work, or at church, I focused only on that. The only areas that had my thoughts at all times were my kids and God. The day I thought I'd give up, I decided instead to go to the Psychology Department and get the help I needed to finish my journey. Compartmentalizing my life and getting help allowed me to graduate and become an author and a radio and TV host, and to raise three wonderful children.

You may have several things you are working on day after day. Your classwork, a part-time job, extracurricular activities, chores at home, and community events can all put a demand on your time and thoughts. Like me, you also must learn to be present for your life. Giving something your undivided attention helps you to be your best. On the other hand, not being present robs you and others of the experience that should be realized in that moment. Now that's winning!

PERSONAL
TOUCH!

By Letitia Thornhill

Celebrity Makeup Artist
CEO, LetBeauty, LLC
Featured artist, BET, TV One, ABC, C-Span, *Sister to Sister
Magazine*, *DC Modern Magazine*, Miss USA, Miss Teen
Pageants, and Fond Memories with Portrait Artist Jackie Hicks
www.theletbeauty.com

As a little girl, I knew exactly what I wanted to do. I knew if I was to be a successful makeup artist, I needed to *Follow My Dreams*. Following my dreams allowed me to embellish such celebrities as Kerry Washington, Tre Songz, Phylicia Rashad, Laylah Hathaway, Eric Bennett, Wayne Brady, Free, Venus and Serena Williams, Michelle Williams from Destiny's Child, and many more.

Choosing to work in my *passion over a paycheck* (opting to do what I love over money) has also been a big factor in my success. It has allowed me to work with some amazing people and to give back to the community through various outreach organizations, programs, and classes.

The last if not the most important thing that has driven me to have a peak performance is my love for teaching celebrities and the everyday woman that *Beauty is from the Inside Out*. I learned this lesson as my sister battled cancer. She passed away from Hodgkin's lymphoma at the tender age of 21. Throughout her painful journey, I spent precious moments making her glamorous. My ability to make her look and feel beautiful taught me the healing benefits of makeup and how it can be used as a form of outward and inward therapy.

As you strive toward your peak performance, remember to follow your dreams. Do what you absolutely love, and choose your *passion over a paycheck*, knowing that the money will come. Also, let makeup enhance you, not cover you, and always remember that beauty is from the inside out. Live in this truth, and soon you will find your personal touch!

DON'T BLOCK
YOUR "BEAUTIFUL"

By Pastor Veda McCoy

Co-Pastor and Executive Pastor,
Judah Christian Center Church
CEO and Founder, Unlock Your Life Enterprises
Principal, Avalon Elementary School
Master's in Education, Supervision and Administration

My journey into education as a career was not traditional. Actually, it started with a chance meeting at a friend's funeral. I was saying goodbye to a beloved musician-extraordinaire when I ran into a friend and colleague. I told her I was graduating from college, and she asked what I was going to do next. I didn't know. I had been a legal secretary for most of my adult life, but I was looking for more. She asked me if I ever thought about teaching. I had not; however, I was open to it. She setup an interview for me, and I got the job the same day. Later, I became certified for teaching, and earned my master's degree and certification by New Leaders New School, a national training program for principals. I'm so glad I didn't *Block My "Beautiful"*!

Although I didn't set out to be an educator, I consider it a beautiful thing. After all, I get to use my gifts, talents, and abilities to make a difference in the lives of thousands of children, work with some amazing people, and receive training from some of the best educational minds of this generation. I've grown as a leader, executive pastor, and entrepreneur, and I'm able to combine passion and purpose with destiny and calling. I pray the same for you.

You'll never know all life has in store for you, but *don't block your own beautiful!* Never compete with anyone, never compare yourself to anyone, and never complain. I often say, "Complain about nothing and worry about even less." Instead, concentrate on being your #1 fan and letting your personal beauty shine through.

POSITION YOURSELF TO SUCCEED

Affirmation

Today, I position myself to succeed. I will walk in love, integrity, and the power of grace. I commit to giving 100 percent with a personal touch that sets my brand apart from others. I am consistently looking for ways to let my beauty shine forth. I will remain focused, effectively manage my priorities, and maintain a positive attitude as I move toward my dreams. God has an incredible plan for my life. I will be in the right place at the right time with the right people doing the right thing. I give myself permission to be successful and receive nothing but God's best for my life.

_____

_____

_____

_____

_____

_____

_____

_____

_____

_____

_____

_____

_____

_____

PART THREE

MAKE DECISIONS
THAT COUNT

"Once you make a decision,
the universe conspires to make it happen."
~Ralph Waldo Emerson

DON'T LET ANYONE
STEAL YOUR SHINE!

By Keenya Kersey

Fashion Designer
www.georgiastitch.com
contact@georgiastitch.com

In life, you have to learn that the opinions of others are small in comparison to what God thinks of you. God created you, and He has a special plan for your life. He didn't create you to shrink, but to shine, baby girl, shine! You are filled with gifts and talents that the world needs to see. These are not for you to hide under a rock or throw a cover over to keep them from being seen. It's just the opposite. These are your personal sparkles that separate you from the rest. They come to your aid when things get tough and you feel like shrinking back. Instead, *shift into your gift*. It's the one thing that doesn't need anyone's permission for it to happen. It's the one thing that always allows you to simply *"be."*

Someone once said, "At the darkest of night is the brightest of light." So, let your challenges and naysayers (people who don't understand you and those who would rather you play small) be a reminder that it's time to shine. God has given you the ability to be and do anything you want to in life, and your light, when turned on, will shine forth on the path you must take to your brilliance. Yes, this means you may not fit in, can't dress and do what others do, or have to put in extra hours cultivating your gift, but remember that your path is unique and waiting on you to shine bright like a diamond.

EMBRACE IT. OWN IT.
LIVE IT.

By Angel Livas

President, DC Media Connection
DCMediaConnection.com
Gracie Award Winning Producer of Radio Documentary
Member, Board of Governors, The City Club of Washington
Founder, Foundation of Freedom Project

DC Media Connection Named Most Acclaimed Woman-Owned and -Operated Media Startup

"When You Realize Your Passion Suits You …
Wear It Out!" —Angel Livas

Have you discovered that one quirk about yourself that everyone either admires or hates? For most of us, we have various skills, but we always have one talent that is completely effortless. This talent is the one ability that, I believe, God instills in each of us to help us fulfill our life's purpose. When you're seeking to understand your purpose, I encourage you to set aside time to meditate and reflect on your innate gifts. Ask yourself these three questions:

1) What am I most passionate about?
2) What's something that I enjoy doing that feels like "work" to others?
3) In what area of my life do people constantly take notice of my skills and abilities?

Usually, your purpose can be found somewhere between your passion and the one thing at which you're just "a natural!" For me, it's my aptness to connect with others. At a young age, I discovered my "gift of gab" and an effortless ability to engage and build rapport with strangers. As I matured, I realized the power of my gift. Once you identify your God-given talent, embrace it, own it, live it. If you do, you'll be unstoppable.

Thank you for your support. Angel Livas

CHOSEN
TO SLAY
By Shakeita Boyd, B.S.

Founder and CEO, Lavish Life, LLC
Lavishlifesalonmd@gmail.com

Calling all Princesses! Yes, that's you! Not because you believe in fairy tales, but because your Father is the King—God Himself. Just because you are a princess doesn't mean you won't have your share of valley experiences. You may feel defeated, even after you've taken your best shot, or a relationship may test you after you've proven your loyalty. Regardless of the situation, you must remain encouraged. It is in moments like these that you will realize what you're made of. What's inside of you is always greater than the chaos around you. The key to winning here is to have a strategy that will always lead you to your own "Amazing."

How do you get there?

First, recognize that you are chosen. Being chosen is an indication that you are qualified and favored, which places you ahead of the game.

Secondly, you have to adapt successfully in the face of adversity, even if it means changing your current position.

Finally, you must have the confidence and resilience that give you permission to slay any obstacles or perceived competition.

Instead of giving up prematurely on your hopes and dreams, embrace the notion that you are a daughter of the King, and it's in your DNA to slay.

Now, repeat after me:

"I'm far from being mediocre!
I am lavish and, oh, so fabulous!
I am a daughter of the King, a princess,
and yes, I've come to slay!"

YOUR THRONE
AWAITS!

— By Kimberly "Kimbo" Person —

Two-times Innovation Award Recipient
2010 Employee of the Year
Daycare Center Co-Owner
Community Activist
Relations Specialist
Actress in Feature Films

Treating yourself like a "Queen" is one of the necessities of life that comes with major responsibilities. A queen must confidently walk in her authority, protect her legacy, be conscious of her presence, serve the wellbeing of others, be aware of pending issues, serve with grace and poise, and rule her court with love. She respects herself and others, and sets high standards for her life. Her behavior teaches people how to respect her in return. And no, it's not always easy to lead in such a manner, but she knows that it comes with the throne. A queen seeks the council of others, but doesn't compromise her soul, faith, or beliefs. She stays focused on her assignment and ignores the naysayers, knowing that they will be the same people who will need her in the future.

As you grow in your role as Queen, challenges will come, but you must determine the best course of action and assess the risks. Are you taking your education seriously? Are those around you empowering you or bringing you down? Is your attitude helping or hindering your progress?

To rule with majesty, you will need to be disciplined and make sacrifices that others aren't willing to make. It's your responsibility to protect the throne and to maximize your impact on the world. Don't worry, you can do it. You were born to do it. I am not challenging you to step up to your throne because I lived my entire life this way; I'm challenging you to do it because I wish I had discovered my throne much earlier in life. I have it now, and I believe you already have everything you need to take your throne today.

DESTINY
DECISIONS

—By Lakisha M. Pingshaw, CPM—

Broadband Services Manager and Program Manager for
Prince George's County Government,
Office of Information Technology
www.LakishaPingshaw.com

There's a saying, "To every action, there's a reaction." I like to say, "For every decision, there's a consequence, whether good or bad." Choosing your actions doesn't mean you can choose or control the consequences of those actions. Let *that* be the reason you make "destiny decisions." Destiny decisions are the ones tied directly to your destiny. They can be the decisions you make each day. Spend time each day visualizing the destiny you want, because you have to see it and believe it to receive it. Where there is no vision, there is no hope, so make your destiny a part of your everyday language.

Don't let the business of life rob you of the time you need to think, and educate yourself so you can make destiny decisions. Let your destiny decisions dictate who your friends are, determine how you save and spend your money, drive you away from conflict and negativity, and regulate how you spend your precious time. Keep in mind, it won't just happen. You must be deliberate, intentional, and focused on making the right choices for your life.

With your future ahead of you and your past behind you, you will always have a destiny decision to make. It's yours to make. It's yours to claim. Most importantly, it's eagerly awaiting your arrival.

A PEAK
PERFORMANCE

By Jacqueline Hicks

CEO, Fond Memories Photography
First African-American Woman to Win Maryland State
Portrait Photographer of the Year
Master Craftsmen Degree and Photography Degree,
the Professional Photographers of America

Member, Wedding and Portrait Photographers International, the Professional Photographers of America, and the Maryland Professional Photographers Association
Lecturer and Instructor

As time passes, memories are all that remain—precious memories, those that capture the emotion of life's events through portraits. As a world-renowned photographer, capturing treasured moments is my business and at the heart of what I do. Behind my lens, *I Dare to Dream.* I aim high and set elevated standards for myself. I hold myself and my team accountable and give my clients an unforgettable experience.

Next, *I Nurture the Gift.* Not only have I received a Master Craftsmen Degree in Photography, but I also continue to learn and perfect my gift daily. As a young lady, it's important to acknowledge your God-given talents and to educate yourself. This can be done in a formal classroom setting, the virtual classroom, or through an apprenticeship. Empower yourself to develop your skills so you can deliver a peak performance.

To have a peak performance, *I Accept Challenges.* To some, my job looks glamorous. However, it can be filled with challenges and opportunities for me to grow. As an African-American woman, it was not easy for me to enter the male-dominated world of photography. I accepted the challenge, which gave me the fuel to study longer, work harder, and play bigger so I could thrive, soar, and be who I am today.

As a young lady, you will have challenges and trials, but in your challenges and trials, you will find your power, wisdom, knowledge, and understanding. Do not despise or run from challenges. Instead, allow them to propel you in the direction of your dreams. Stay strong, dare to be different, and no matter what, deliver *a peak performance.*

YOUR DATA IS NOT
YOUR DESTINY

By Kimberly E. Gilchrist

Founder and Owner, First Impressions Etiquette
and Charm School, LLC
www.firstimpressionsetiquette.org

In elementary school, I struggled to be in the same league with the visibly smart kids. I tried to hide a learning disability and refused to claim it. I even convinced myself all was good and no one would ever find out. After all, I was the granddaughter of a very prominent Washington, DC, socialite who was enrolled in the Sears Discovery Charm School. My role was to be cute, intelligent, poised, and polished while attending various community activities. I was well on my way to becoming a beautiful debutante, but the beast, dyslexia, kept trying to shatter my dreams. I even had to repeat the second grade.

In high school, I had an awesome mentor who gave me tips on how to manage the disability. Immediately, I decided my data would not be my destiny. I stopped running from it, learned everything I could about it, and worked hard to overcome its characteristics. I accepted the fact that I had to work harder to be successful. As a result of the hard work, I skipped the 11th grade, attended college, and earned my B.S. and Master's degrees.

I encourage you to take charge of your destiny and be your *Best You*. Don't allow old data to dictate your future. Your future is a nest of possibilities. It will look like your past, if you don't choose to press the delete key and give the world an update.

"The only person you are destined to become is
the person you decide to be."
~ *Ralph Waldo Emerson*

THE RIGHT "NOT"
TO REMAIN SILENT

—By Pastor Angela Hood Marshall—

Pastor, Disciples of Christ Holiness Church
Founder and CEO, Life Unlocked

"She's ugly, stinky, bony, poor, or a black sheep." "She will never amount to anything." "She will always be a boyfriend stealer."

"Is this me?" "Are they right?" "Am I what they say I am?"

Sticks and stones may break your bones, but we all know that words really do hurt! Like others, I allowed people to speak ill of me while I remained silent. Then one day, I spoke up! I decided that I am not who they say I am. I'm not ugly! I'm not a reject! I am somebody, even when I make mistakes in life! I am who God says I am!

I spoke up for myself. I challenge you to do the same. Find the confidence within to speak up for yourself. Love yourself enough to open your mouth, declare blessings over your entire life, and refuse to be silent.

What happens is that people peek in and see where they believe God is taking you, and they become afraid of who you will be, and rightfully so. God created a masterpiece when He created you, and I challenge you to accept it, grow in it, and go forward! You are beautiful! You are gifted! You are more than you could ever think.

Even though the words hurt, I didn't allow them to stop me, and neither will you. I learned that I had the right to *not* be silent. Through my struggles of being molested and teenage pregnancy, I vowed to be better. I vowed to be successful. I vowed to make a difference in this Earth. I vowed to no longer be silent. I gave myself *permission to win* by giving myself *permission to speak!*

BOOKS AND BOYS
DON'T MIX

By Thelia Buchanan

Certified Professional Coach
Excellence in Leadership Award Recipient from the Women's
Leadership and Development Institute Alumnae
Mentor and Facilitator, Debs In Christ, Redirecting Delinquent
Youth, and Just Plain Manners Institute

PERMISSION TO WIN

Teens in Action Life Skills Instructor
Coordinator, Catholic Charities–Project Prepare Program

I was the eldest child of a divorced mother of four and my grandma's first grand baby, so I was not only to represent my family well, but also to represent myself well as a female—these were high expectations. I often heard my grandmother say, "Boys and books don't mix," and my mother would "cosign" in the background. Often over breakfast before I headed off to school, they would say, "Remember, Thelia, boys and books don't mix," as if I was running off to the boys' locker room. They would also say it whenever I was to be in a situation where a boy just might also be. Although I'm making light of it now, I realized that it was their way of helping me stay focused on what was really important—my goals. Yes, it was wonderful to have the looks that caused guys to notice me from time to time, but it was more important to have the smarts.

Setting goals and staying focused were a sure win for me. In high school and college, I had the honor roll certificates and all kinds of ribbons of achievement as proof of my hard work, and I continued to accomplish even more in graduate school. I must admit, staying focused and in the books got tough sometimes, but now, with a grin, I say "Thank you, Mom and Grandma, for reminding me of the expectations. I made it."

Did you know failing to take care of your education today will limit your opportunities tomorrow, including the caliber of nice young men who could be interested in you?

MAKE DECISIONS THAT COUNT

Today, I embrace, own, and live in my truth. I refuse to let anyone steal my shine or cause me to derail my divine destiny. I choose to slay opposition and operate at the highest peak. As queen, I arise with grace to my throne with gentle care for myself and others. I freely let go of all energies and distractions, including boys who come to alter my journey to success. I refuse to be silent and let the things of the past overshadow my bright, brilliant, and bodacious future. I give myself permission to seek the wisdom, knowledge, and understanding I need to make healthy choices for my life.

_____
_____
_____
_____
_____
_____
_____
_____
_____
_____
_____
_____
_____
_____

PART FOUR

PRESS INTO YOUR PROMISE

"Success in life is a matter not so much of talent or opportunity as of concentration and perseverance."
~ C. W. Wendte

DON'T
"QUUIT"

By Felicia Vice

Independent Sales Director, Mary Kay Cosmetics
www.marykay.com/fvice

Did you know that you are unique—fearfully and wonderfully made by God. God chose you to be who you are! He has a specific plan for your life that only you can fulfill. Refuse to give up on life, school, and, most importantly, yourself. You are your biggest investment.

I started my journey as an Independent Beauty Consultant with Mary Kay Cosmetics 13 years ago, with a dream of joining the Top 2 percent of my company. Having experienced numerous setbacks, I almost gave up on myself and on my dream. You see, I didn't think I was good enough or smart enough; and frankly, I almost didn't believe that I deserved such an honor. Once I learned who God created me to be and realized that it was more than enough to accomplish my wildest dreams, I decided never again to QUUIT (Question Ur Unique & Incredible Transformation). As a result of finding the courage to believe in myself, believe in my dreams, and believe that I deserved to have God's best, I accomplished my dream! I became an Independent Sales Director in a company that I simply love. The transformation of my mind, body, and spirit in the process was astounding. Not only did I lose body weight, but I also released unnecessary weights from my mind. My priorities shifted. I attracted a new like-minded community who truly supported me as the best me that I can be.

Now, guess what. You can do the same thing. You can accomplish whatever you want to accomplish, release yourself from all unnecessary weights, and attract a community of other young ladies who also want to soar. It may not appear to be that way right now, but it will happen if you learn to accept your uniqueness and believe everything that God says about you. And whatever you do, just Don't QUUIT! Transformation is on the way!

A PASSION
FOR SUCCESS

By Yvette Acevedo

Independent Sales Director, Mary Kay Cosmetics
www.marykay.com/yacevedo

A winning strategy begins with a belief in oneself. Know that you have within you what it takes to succeed, but it can never be seen or flourish until you begin to live beyond you and share it.

You must first determine what you have a passion for. Once you discover this, go after it with all of your heart. Prepare, plan, and pursue it daily. Let that passion fuel you every step of the way. Tell it "good morning," take it with you throughout the day, escort it back home, and tuck it in each night. Never let it out of your sight. Your passion will differentiate you from everyone else.

Along the way, you will stumble, but that's all part of the process. Keep "becoming." Search long and hard to learn something new along the way. Every obstacle is an opportunity waiting to be revealed. Keep learning the lessons, and keep kicking the disappointments to the curb. Embrace it all as part of your incredible journey, knowing that in the end, it will strengthen you in ways you could never have imagined.

Lastly, surround yourself with like-minded people who support your dreams and challenge you to grow. You will become like the people you spend the most time with, so choose wisely.

Today you stand as the CEO of your life. Use your passion to generate the success that you envision deep inside.

NEVER
GIVE UP

—By Aquanetta J. Betts, Esquire—

Founder, Law Office of Aquanetta J. Betts, LLC
www.AbettsLaw.com

Some people are born with a silver spoon to get them ahead in many areas of life. If you are like me, you had no such luck or resources. Instead, I was raised in a family that valued hard work and expected me to respect others and take responsibility for my actions. These values are priceless. However, three little words have made a huge difference in my life: *Never give up.*

No careers, businesses, or creations happen overnight or without obstacles and setbacks. Thus, you must always remember to persevere, be tenacious, and stay persistent when pursuing your dreams or anything of great importance to you. Success is yours to claim! You have to want it badly enough to go after it.

When life gets tough, simply get tougher. When the load gets heavy, brace yourself and find ways to lighten the load or share it with someone who supports you. Don't be afraid to ask for help or to create opportunities for others to partner with you. When you don't see an answer in sight, believe that an answer is on the way. Whatever you do face or hear that challenges you, let it do what it does, but don't you give up. "Never, Ever, Ever Give Up" should be your anthem in life.

CHASING THAT
DREAM

By Dominique Brown

Actress
International Student, London England

"If you want something you've never had, you've got to do something you've never done" —Unknown

When I decided I was going to travel halfway around the world to London so I could study classical acting and train in the greatest city at one of the top schools in the world, I wasn't sure about the concept. I knew I would have to make a move to advance me in the direction of my goal to be a working actress. Something had to change, and it needed to be drastic to shake me out of my comfort zone. I soon received confirmation that I could never succeed if I was afraid of failure. I had to get uncomfortable to chase my dream.

You will also have to get uncomfortable to chase your dream. This means letting go of people who say "You can't do it," or "You're crazy." It means shutting down that little voice inside you that speaks negatively out of fear. It means accepting that your growth lies beyond your comfort zone. Therefore, remember to:

1) Dream your dream.
2) Consciously decide to pursue it, despite the fears.
3) Ask for help.
4) Stay on track.
5) Keep your head high; make revisions if need be.
6) Share your journey.
7) Go for it!

You never know who needs to hear your story. Your journey may not always be smooth sailing, but things will work out. If you hit a roadblock, keep a level head and think of new ways to accomplish what you set out to do.

MISSION
"I'M POSSIBLE"

By Verna Robinson

Project Director, LMCi
Over 20 Years in Government Contracting

You are on the mission of a lifetime! You have been assigned to protect a precious jewel. You must keep it out of harm's way. You cannot let any negative, outside forces try to devalue or destroy it. You must understand that this jewel is priceless. It's more precious than all the diamonds in the world. It's truly one of a kind. This unique jewel was made to be honored and praised. It was placed here to do great things and was birthed through purpose.

Your mission, should you choose to accept it, is to realize that *you are the precious jewel.*

Yes, it's you! You are a special jewel that God's own Hands made, created to shine bright and win big. You were made by Greatness for greatness, and you should be honored, respected, and valued as such. You are full of possibilities and power; thus, the heights to where you can soar are endless.

Will you accept this mission and come to terms with your unique brilliance?

This mission at times may seem to be impossible, but it's not. You must constantly remind yourself that it's possible because *"I'm possible."* It's possible to achieve layers and layers of new possibilities, but you must put a demand on your potential. It's possible to spring forth to fulfill all of your dreams and goals, but you must believe you deserve them.

Remember to believe the mission is possible, because *"I'm possible."* Keep working hard at achieving your goals, be great at what you do, and give yourself *permission to win* by proving … *I'm possible!*

PERSISTENCE
AND BELIEF
By Shayna Calandro

Journalist, On-Air Personality, and
Sport and Entertainment Reporter
Howard University Alumna, 2014
ShaynaCalandro.com

To grow into the woman you are meant to be, no matter what career path you choose, you will need to be persistent and believe you can do anything you set your mind to do. To be persistent means to continue firmly or obstinately in a course of action despite difficulty or opposition, and to endure over time. People along the way will try to tell you that you can't do it, or you aren't good enough for this or that. However, one of the greatest lessons you can learn is how to feed off negativity. You can't stop it, so you might as well use it to your advantage. If you don't learn how to feed off it, you will end up drowning in it. Besides, negative people have a very important role in the scheme of things. They can be your greatest motivation. Let them fuel you to work harder, dream bigger, and push well past the goal you set.

Believing in yourself also helps you be persistent and makes the process of achieving your dreams that much easier. The truth is, if you don't believe in yourself, nobody else will. Think of a plan to execute your goals and write the plan down; then each day do something that will help you execute the plan. Don't let yourself off the hook. In the long run, your continuous hard work will be noticed, even if it seems not to be recognized at first. Keep pushing toward success, soaring over every obstacle, and slam-dunking your goals.

EXALTATION!

By Lauraline Gregory

Retired Senior Executive Service in the Federal Government
Graduate, University of Maryland University College

Be courageous about your desires that God has placed in your heart. These bold and fierce passions energize you and keep you moving full-steam ahead, so don't hold back waiting for the perfect opportunity. Many times, opportunities appear as detours to position you better for the perfect opportunity. For example, it may be necessary to go to a community college to become prepared for the university of your choice, but don't get discouraged and lose sight of the bigger picture. Believe that you can do it, and you'll be everything you want to be.

As a native of Washington, DC, I graduated from a vocational high school, because I always wanted to be an Executive Secretary—not just any secretary, but an Executive Secretary. After high school, I went to college at night and became a secretary in the Federal Government to pay for it. Afterwards, I graduated from UMUC and participated in some of the country's best leadership programs, such as Sloane Business School at MIT and JFK School of Business at Harvard University. Then it happened. I accepted an elite Senior Executive Service position making a six-figure salary.

God's desires for me surpassed my desires for myself. Those desires you have that won't go away, your belief that God will never fail you, and maintaining a grateful spirit every step of the way will propel you to His perfect plan for your life. Be prepared to praise Him every step of the way, and be blessed!

THE RESOLVE
TO WIN

By Michelle Reese-Wiseman

Owner and Principal Mortician,
Wiseman Funeral Home and Chapel
Graduate, Mortuary College
www.wisemanfuneralhome.net

Life is a splendid thing. However, I realized early on that life makes no promises. Additionally, the reliance on a human to rescue or aid you is a very futile exercise. It is my desire to be successful in life. Because the drive to succeed must be fresh for me every day, I make a conscience decision to win ... *everyday!* My focus is rarely on the emotions or circumstances of the here and now. I try to remain focused on the wonderful, endless possibilities of the future. Therefore, almost everything I do, many of the words I speak, and almost every decision I make is juxtaposed against or compared to the glittering lure of my dreams.

My dreams are bolstered by something much larger than myself. I like to refer to this intangible entity as *hope*. Hope is the vehicle that allows me to *fearlessly* advance, step by step, toward my goals. Hope is the fuel that produces *tenacity*. Tenacity is a great mental and spiritual muscle builder; once employed, it has the ability to catapult you into your wildest dreams. My hope is also derived from the value I place on winning.

Your dreams are huge, so your hopes need to be high. Take nothing for granted, however. Even when you're uncertain, never let it prevent you from forging fearlessly ahead. Fully expect to take your rightful place in the seat of success, and release the fear. Be tenacious, and press through your struggles until you see the success you desire.

STEP BY
STEP!

By Krista Woods

Inventor and CEO, GloveStix
Winner of NBC's TODAY Show's "Next Big Thing"
QVC's "Saturday Morning Q®" Broadcast
Featured in *The Washington Business Journal,*
Fortune Magazine, and *The Washington Post*

Have you ever left your house in the morning on your way to work or maybe to a friend's house? Nothing very stressful about that journey; you've been there before, and you know the way. Heck, you probably know four different ways just in case there's traffic or a road closure. You need to have options, because you never know when something will try to prevent you from reaching your destination. Well, imagine that friend lives across the country. Imagine there are no road maps, Google, or smart phones for that matter. Pretty scary thought, right? So, now what? You know where you want to be, and you know in what direction to go. You get together the best plan you can and take that first step out the door! That's where it all starts, that first step. You know what's next? The second step. The same thing applies with your life's journey—that big idea, that thing you've always wanted to do, that business you want to start, or that life you want to live. *The "Big" dream! The "Wouldn't it be Amazing! Unbelievable! Unthinkable!" dream.* Yes, *that* dream!

Here's the secret: Your dreams will always be just dreams until you decide to take that first step. You get there by moving toward it, and then you adapt, adjust, and overcome every single roadblock, detour, 70-foot wall, or fire-breathing dragon that stands in your way. You do it whether you're happy, angry, frustrated, or scared. Whatever rollercoaster of emotions it takes you on, just keep moving and watch the beauty of the journey unfold in front of you and for you. Those priceless discoveries are the only guarantees you have. Until then, your dream will forever be just a dream. Continue to dream step by step.

PRESS INTO YOUR PROMISE

Affirmation

Today, I press forward into the promises of God for my life. I refuse to give up or quit on His precious plans for me. With passions ever burning, I chase those dreams and accomplish my unique mission. I can, I shall, I will persevere, believing I can accomplish anything I set my mind to do. To increase my resolve to win, step by step I'll overcome all challenges. I give myself permission to take hold of everything that is good, perfect, and worthy of praise.

PART FIVE

UNCOVER HIDDEN TREASURES

*"Nothing is a waste of time
if you use the experience wisely."
~ Auguste Rodin*

FORTUNATE
MISTAKES

By Sharnita L. Smith

Health and Fitness Motivator
Elementary Teacher
Graduate, Great North Carolina Central University

Everyone makes mistakes. The good fortune comes when you discover the treasures that lie inside your mistakes. Finding these jewels will help you to doubt less and pray more. Instead of questioning yourself because of past experiences, you can give yourself the credit for realizing what you've done, and then use it as a building block to your next level. This doesn't mean you should be careless about your choices; instead, you should be careful about them. This means learning from moments of error and using them to mature your patience, strengthen your faith, and increase your knowledge and determination to win.

I learned this lesson a few years back when I weighed close to 300 pounds. I didn't take care of my body, which led to deep depression. I was in a really dark place, and I soon realized that my obesity was killing me. That's when I began to pray about my situation. I saw where I was making major mistakes and not loving myself enough to take care of the issues causing my obesity. I found scriptures that gave me strength to change my eating habits, and I started working out. Within a year, I had lost 100 pounds.

Today, I'm preparing to compete in a Female Figure Bodybuilding Competition. I've also used the lessons I learned to create a Women's Fitness and Wellness Program and a clothing line. Just like that, you can find priceless fortunes in your mistakes that will cause you to soar to your next level.

FIND A MENTOR
TO HELP YOU REACH
FOR THE STARS

By Janice Hallé

CEO, Flexflop
Flexflop.com

I started in the high-tech industry in the early 1980s when it was predominately a man's world. I struggled for a while to navigate my way through uncharted waters, but it wasn't until I sought out a mentor, someone who had years of experience in the same field, that things changed for me.

A great mentor will share her experiences and wisdom, and guide you through unfamiliar territory. She can help you set and achieve your goals; she will learn your strengths and weaknesses and push you out of your comfort zone so you can achieve all that you desire.

Mentors may span a wide range of topics, such as growing as leader, providing personal insight, building your skills, or increasing your academic and professional performance. I have had many mentors over the years, and I know they believed in me and gave me the confidence and encouragement that I needed to have a very successful 31-year career as an engineer. Today, I derive great pleasure in mentoring young women and hope to give back all that was given to me.

Look around to see who would be an incredible mentor for you. Simply share with them your desire to work together, and be willing to make a significant investment of time, energy, and resources. When done right, it can be a powerful experience for both of you.

THE LEGACY OF
FAMILY
—— *By Harriet Carr Hart* ——

Honored Mother, Grandmother, and Great-Grandmother
Recipient, 2015 Dorothy M. Hart Woman of Legacy Award for
Her Exceptional Walk of Love, Compassion, Service,
and Grace

30+ Years at the Howard University Hospital's Family Planning, with Love, Care and Spiritual Guidance

Next to my love for God and my relationship with Him is the love of my life and heart—my family. Family is the most important responsibility with which God has entrusted me. Family is my greatest achievement and my legacy. The quality of family life is crucial to my happiness and emotional well-being, but family needs continuous nurturing and love daily. God values family, calling children "a heritage from the Lord." Families are the foundation of society.

My mother and father had 14 children, and we tried every day to show our love for one another. We were not at all perfect, but our parents taught us how to be grateful and thankful for what we had and to be proud of who we were.

At an early age, I was taught *6 important values of a loving family*, which I live by today, have instilled in my family, and share with you. They are: 1) stay committed, 2) show your appreciation for one another, 3) communicate openly, 4) spend time together, 5) lift up each other, extending a hand, and 6) continue to grow in your spiritual well-being.

Most importantly, I say to you, read the Bible every day and apply it to your everyday needs. Don't hesitate to ask God for guidance, and understand that He knows what's best and will guide you into all Truth.

Meditate on *Proverbs 3:5-6* and *Proverbs 4:7*. Keep these Scriptures close to your heart, and you will be proud of your family heritage.

LOVE
A SISTAH

By Authoress Tonya Wilson

B.A. Degree, Towson University
Member of Delta Sigma Theta Sorority, Inc.
Featured Author, "Deltas on Tour," 2015–2017
Published Author of Four Books in 2015
Recipient of African-American Author's Award, 2016
Retired Member of U.S. Army Reserves

Radio Host and Producer, "Word Up," W646, Queen City Bullies Radio, Charlotte, NC

In this lifetime, so much hatred, envy, and strife exist among women, but I have discovered that we are all fighting for the same things: love, harmony, security, peace, joy, stability, true friendship, and the favor of God.

At one time, all we had was each other; the color of our skin and a common cause united us. Today, we appear to be like crabs in a pot of hot water, pulling one another down instead of up and out of a negative situation. You might not think so, but when we gossip about our sister—or "sistah"—slander her name, bully her, or covet her possessions, including her boyfriend or husband, we are doing just that.

I encourage you, my sistah, to stand up and be the true winner you are. This starts with loving yourself so that you can sincerely love another sistah. Let your character be Christ-like in all your ways. This doesn't mean you must be perfect, but it does mean that you must be considerate of one another in your daily walk.

You never know what another sistah is going through. Just because she is smiling doesn't mean that everything is wonderful. You might be the person God wants to encourage her and lift her spirits that day. You just don't know. Your gentle touch may remind her that she's not alone and get her through a difficult time. Your smile might be the only sunshine she sees that day. Again, you just never know.

Whatever the case may be, there is hope for us all. Keep a sistah in your heart each day, and wear your smile like a priceless crown. This is truly what the world needs. Believe me, it's contagious!

BEST FRIENDS AND FAITH (BFFs)

—By Dr. Rosalind S. Brathwaite—

Associate Pastor, Grace Evangelical Lutheran Church
Honorary Doctorate of Divinity, Martha's Vineyard
Theological Seminary
Graduate, Lutheran Theological Seminary, Philadelphia, PA
B.A. Degree, College of New Rochelle
President, Black Pastors Group and Urban Leaders Institute

Looking back over my life, I've come to realize the importance of BFFs (best friends forever). My teen years gave me a broader look at the world around me. I clung to my faith and my friends. At the age of 15, the Lord called me to serve Him and others by joining the church and teaching Sunday School. At the same time, I was introduced to school integration and was bussed to an all-white high school outside my neighborhood. Until then, I had always attended schools with all Black students and White teachers. I had no idea about the challenges I was about to face.

As a pioneer of integration, life became a series of obstacles to overcome. I was placed in an environment where I was not wanted. My prior educational system had not prepared me to meet the standards that the White students had achieved. I was setup to fail, but my faith in God gave me the courage to press on, knowing that He would get me through it and help me overcome.

Thankfully, two of my BFFs whom I met in the second grade had also been bussed to the new school. The challenges actually knitted us together. We built a bond that helped us survive really rough times. This 70-year friendship is stronger today, and so is our faith. With God, *all* things are possible. Open your heart and He will send you true friends to make your journey easier, help you grow, and share the real love of Christ through the friendship. True BFFs—Best Friends and Faith—are invaluable.

UNCOVER HIDDEN TREASURES

Today, I embrace the privilege of learning from my mistakes. I am wiser now and more confident in the road I must take. I appreciate the true sisterhood that surrounds me, and I let go of those who do not mean me any good. My faith in God gives me joy in knowing that all things are working together for my good, whether I realize it or not. I have no more hesitations or fear, but instead I draw unto me the love, support, and dedication of my family and friends. I give myself permission to uncover and receive the treasures that mentors, positive situations, and opportunities will afford me.

GLOSSARY

Amazing	Causing great surprise or wonder, astonishing; startlingly impressive
Aspirations	A strong desire to achieve something high or great; an object of such desire
Attitude	The way you think and feel about someone or something; a feeling or way of thinking that affects a person's behavior
Branding	To develop a unique professional identity and coherent message that sets you apart from others either in your company or in your industry; a particular kind or type of something
Brilliance	Great brightness; luster: the brilliance of a fine diamond; excellence or distinction; conspicuous talent, mental ability, etc.
Chosen	Having been selected as the best or most appropriate
Consistent	Always acting or behaving in the same way; of the same quality; especially: good each time; continuing to happen or develop in the same way

Destiny
: The events that will necessarily happen to a particular person or thing in the future: what happens in the future: the things that someone or something will experience in the future

Dreams
: A series of thoughts, visions, or feelings that happen during sleep; an idea or vision that is created in your imagination and that is not tangible or in the present; something that you have wanted very much to do, be, or have for a long time

Exaltation
: The act of raising someone or something in importance: the act of exalting someone or something or the state of being exalted; a strong sense of happiness, power, or importance

Fearless
: Not afraid: very brave; free from F.E.A.R. (False Evidence Appearing Real)

Goal
: The result or achievement toward which effort is directed; aim; end

Honor
: Respect that is given to someone who is admired; good reputation: good quality or character as judged by other people; high moral standards of behavior

Hope
: To want something to happen or be true and think that it could happen or be true; to cherish a desire with anticipation

Indomitable	Impossible to subdue or defeat
Inspire	To make (someone) want to do something: to give (someone) an idea about what to do or create; to cause (something) to happen or be created; to influence, move, or guide by divine or supernatural inspiration; to exert an animating, enlivening, or exalting influence on
Listen	Give one's attention to; to pay attention to someone or something in order to hear what is being said, sung, played, etc.; to hear what someone has said and understand that it is serious, important, or true
Mentor	A person or friend who guides a less experienced person by building trust and modeling positive behaviors, who understands their role is to be dependable, engaged, authentic, and tuned into the needs of the mentee; a trusted counselor or guide
Mission	A pre-established and often self-imposed objective or purpose; a task or job that someone is given to do; a specific task with which a person or a group is charged
Passion	A strong feeling of enthusiasm or excitement for something or about doing something

PERMISSION TO WIN

Permission	The right or ability to do something that is given by someone who has the power to decide if it will be allowed
Perseverance	The quality that allows someone to continue trying to do something even though it is difficult
Persevere	To persist in a state, enterprise, or undertaking in spite of counterinfluences, opposition, or discouragement
Possibility	A chance that something might exist, happen, or be true: the state or fact of being possible
Power	Ability to act or produce an effect; ability to get extra-base hits; capacity for being acted upon or undergoing an effect; legal or official authority, capacity, or right
Reality	The true situation that exists: the real situation; something that actually exists or happens: a real event, occurrence, situation, etc.
Responsibility	The state or fact of having a duty to deal with something or of having control over someone
Sistah	A strong sister with a diva attitude; a girl or woman regarded as a comrade; one that is closely similar to or associated with another

Strategy	A careful plan or method for achieving a particular goal usually over a long period; the skill of making or carrying out plans to achieve a goal
Success	Favorable or desired outcome; the accomplishment of an aim or purpose; the attainment of wealth, favor, or eminence; one that succeeds
Tenacious	Not easily stoppable or severed: firm or strong; continuing for a long time; very determined to do something
Tenacity	The quality or fact of being very determined; determination
Value	A person's principles or standards of behavior; one's judgment of what is important in life
Vision	something seen in the mind (as during a dream); a vivid picture created by the imagination
Win	To achieve victory in a fight, contest, game, etc.; to get (something, such as a prize) by achieving victory in a fight, contest, game, etc.: to get (something) by effort

ABOUT
Kimberly D. Hart

Kimberly D. Hart, The Winning Strategist, is a Licensed Minister, who is known for her ability to motivate and inspire people to play bigger in life. As a sought-after Speaker, Coach, Trainer and Mentor, Kimberly D loves to breathe life back into people, professionals, and organizations that are struggling to grow, reproduce, adapt, perform, and excel.

She is the Founder and CEO of Kimberly D. Hart Consulting & Development Firm, Daughters of Legacy Network, and Queens 2 Bee Mentoring and Development for young ladies. Kimberly provides her clients with the clarity, strategies, tools, and resources they need to be fruitful and live "Amazing" lives.

Kimberly is indeed a "Connector," and she welcomes new opportunities to connect People to their Passion, Purpose, Power, and Profitability.

To learn more about Kimberly D. Hart and her products and services, get connected at:

KimberlyDHart.com

THE DAUGHTERS OF
LEGACY

*Come from out of the shadows of your story
and step into the spotlight of your own destiny.*

The Daughters of Legacy is an elite network of women leaders, professionals, and entrepreneurs committed to connecting and collaborating to achieve goals, leverage strengths, and grow businesses. We achieve this vision by:

- Providing learning opportunities to foster personal and business development
- Providing unique gatherings to foster community
- Strategically aligning businesses and partnerships with others who share our vision and seek to engage professional women
- Providing oversight to Queens 2 Bee Mentoring & Developing Program

- Leveraging skills, influences, and strengths to create a legacy for the next generation of winners

Annually, a special team of women are chosen to represent diverse issues common to women and those growing into their unique womanhood. This team of extraordinary women work together to strengthen the capacity of our sisters to win via one-on-one and group coaching sessions, training forums, virtual presentations, and special events.

PURPOSE ● VISION ● MISSION ● SPIRIT ● WELLNESS
FAMILY ● RELATIONSHIPS ● EDUCATION ● FINANCES
COMMUNICATION ● STYLE ● MINISTRY ● LEADERSHIP
CAREER ● BUSINESS ● ETIQUETTE *

"CREATING A LEGACY … THAT SHALL REMAIN!"

Become a member today at
DaughtersofLegacy.Com

QUEENS 2 BEE
MENTORING AND DEVELOPMENT
FOR YOUNG LADIES

Queens2Bee.com
QUEENS2BEE@GMAIL.COM
FACEBOOK GROUP / TWITTER: QUEENS 2 BEE

*Our mission is to Educate and Empower young ladies to
nurture their positive attributes and
Expose them to possibilities beyond their immediate reach.*

As a faith-based nonprofit organization, we are creating a culture of young ladies who confidently walk in their purpose, lead by example, maximize their potential, and inspire their peers as well as the next generation to live in their amazing. This is achieved by connecting highly motivated young ladies with professional women, customized training, high-quality resources, and one-of-a-kind exposure that support their personal, professional, and leadership development.

If you are a young lady between the ages of 8 and 18 and you are ready to Think Big, Shine Bright...and Grow with other Extraordinary Young Ladies so that you can:

- Become staples of influence in the community
- Set goals and build strategies to chart your success
- Receive individual and group mentoring from professional women across various industries
- Join a cadre of like-minded sisters who are ready to play and win big in life
- Receive incredible rewards and recognition for your accomplishments
- Enter the Royal Court and receive VIP Recognition

... Then QUEENS 2 BEE is for YOU!

Register for one of the programs below at Queens2bee.com

169

NOTES

NOTES